T0311523

Cambridge Elements ☰

Elements in the Philosophy of Physics
edited by
James Owen Weatherall
University of California, Irvine

SPECIAL RELATIVITY

James Read
University of Oxford

CAMBRIDGE
UNIVERSITY PRESS

CAMBRIDGE
UNIVERSITY PRESS

Shaftesbury Road, Cambridge CB2 8EA, United Kingdom

One Liberty Plaza, 20th Floor, New York, NY 10006, USA

477 Williamstown Road, Port Melbourne, VIC 3207, Australia

314–321, 3rd Floor, Plot 3, Splendor Forum, Jasola District Centre,
New Delhi – 110025, India

103 Penang Road, #05–06/07, Visioncrest Commercial, Singapore 238467

Cambridge University Press is part of Cambridge University Press & Assessment,
a department of the University of Cambridge.

We share the University's mission to contribute to society through the pursuit of
education, learning and research at the highest international levels of excellence.

www.cambridge.org
Information on this title: www.cambridge.org/9781009300612
DOI: 10.1017/9781009300599

First published 2023

A catalogue record for this publication is available from the British Library.

ISBN 978-1-009-30061-2 Paperback
ISSN 2632-413X (online)
ISSN 2632-4121 (print)

Special Relativity

Elements in the Philosophy of Physics

DOI: 10.1017/9781009300599
First published online: June 2023

James Read
University of Oxford

Author for correspondence: James Read, james.read@philosophy.ox.ac.uk

Abstract: This Element presents the philosophy of special relativity, from the foundations of the theory in Newtonian mechanics, through its birth out of the ashes of nineteenth-century ether theory, through the various conceptual paradoxes which the theory presents, and finally arriving at some of its connections with Einstein's later theory of general relativity. It illustrates concepts such as inertial frames, force-free motion, dynamical versus geometrical understandings of physics, the standard hierarchy of classical spacetimes, and symmetries of a physical theory; it also discusses specific topics in the foundations of special relativity such as Einstein's 1905 derivation of the Lorentz transformations, the conventionality of simultaneity, the status of frame-dependent effects, and the twin paradox.

Keywords: special relativity, spacetime, Einstein, geometry, dynamics

ISBNs: 9781009300612 (PB), 9781009300599 (OC)
ISSNs: 2632-413X (online), 2632-4121 (print)

Contents

1 Newton's Laws

Sir Isaac Newton (Figure 1) was born in 1642 and died in 1726 or 1727. What? How can there be any ambiguity over something so straightforward as the year of Newton's death? In his time, two calendars were in use in Europe: the Julian 'old style' calendar (introduced by Julius Caesar in 46 BC), and the Gregorian 'new style' calendar (introduced by Pope Gregory XIII in October 1582). While the Julian calendar counts the length of a year as exactly 365.25 days long, meaning a leap year should occur every four years, the Gregorian calendar has the following more sophisticated prescription:

> Every year that is exactly divisible by four is a leap year, except for years that are exactly divisible by 100, but these centurial years are leap years if they are exactly divisible by 400. For example, the years 1700, 1800, and 1900 are not leap years, but the year 2000 is. (US Naval Observatory, 2022)

The Gregorian calendar is now the calendar most widely used across the globe. Unlike the Julian calendar, it makes the average calendar year 365.2425 days long, thereby more closely approximating the 365.2422-day 'solar' year that is determined by the Earth's revolution around the Sun. The merit of the Gregorian over the Julian calendar is that the latter 'drifts' with respect to the solar year (because the Julian calendar does not as accurately line up with the solar year): given enough time, Christmas in the northern hemisphere would occur in summer according to the Julian calendar! One does not face these issues with the Gregorian calendar: in a sense, it is better 'adapted' to salient physical events (in this case, the Earth's going around the Sun); in turn, this often renders its descriptions of physical goings-on simpler (for example, the Earth will be at the same point in its orbit around the sun every year according to the Gregorian calendar, but not according to the Julian calendar). To anticipate some terminology which I will use later in this section: there is a sense in which the Gregorian calendar better approximates an 'inertial frame' – a coordinatisation of the world such that our description of physical dynamics is simplest – than does the Julian calendar.[1]

In fact, a central question in the philosophy of spacetime physics has to do with precisely these issues: What does it *mean* for our physical descriptions to be 'well-adapted' to nature? Is it indeed appropriate (as assumed so far in this Element) to regard 'inertial frames' as those in which physical dynamics simplifies maximally, or is there some other, superior way of understanding such structures – perhaps in terms of the structures of space and time themselves?

---

[1] Of course the Gregorian calendar is not perfect either: this is why we must introduce 'leap seconds' and other gadgetry in order to forestall 'drift' against the solar year.

Figure 1 Sir Isaac Newton, 1642–1726/7

These are pressing questions, to which I will return throughout this Element – but they are also tangible questions: the entire set of ideas underlying them is encapsulated in the ambiguity over Newton's death year.

My purpose in this section is to expand upon these central themes in the foundations of spacetime theories, as they constitute the essential bedrock upon which I will build my philosophical analysis of special relativity in later sections. In order to proceed, I will turn again to Newton: this time not to his death date, but rather to his *laws*. These turn out to be a conceptual minefield – but grappling with how to understand the content of these laws will afford exactly the right toolkit with which to address the philosophy of special relativity in later sections.[2]

1.1 Newton's Laws

Let me begin by stating Newton's laws. These should be familiar to anyone who has studied high school physics:

N1L: Force-free bodies travel with uniform velocity.

N2L: The total force on a body is equal to the product of that body's mass and its acceleration. ($\mathbf{F} = m\mathbf{a}$.)

N3L: Action and reaction are equal in magnitude and opposite in direction – that is, if one body exerts a force $\mathbf{F}$ on a second body, then the second exerts a force $-\mathbf{F}$ on the first.

---

[2] In many respects, this first section will be the hardest of the Element, because I will introduce a large number of concepts and issues in quite short succession. But readers should not be deterred: I will go into all such concepts and issues in much greater depth in the remaining sections.

Stare at these laws for just a minute, and inevitably a range of conceptual questions will arise. For example:

1. What does 'force-free' mean?
2. Is not **N1L** a special case of **N2L**? So why state it as a separate law?
3. (Relatedly:) Is **N1L** supposed to be a definition, or something else?
4. In which frames of reference are these laws supposed to hold?
5. Does **N1L** presuppose **N3L**?

Only by answering such questions can we secure a full and clear understanding of the content of Newton's laws. But doing so has long been recognised to be no easy business. Here is Hertz in 1894:

> It is quite difficult to present the introduction to mechanics to an intelligent audience without some embarrassment, without the feeling that one should apologize here and there, without the wish to pass quickly over the beginnings. (Hertz, 1894)

And here is the physicist Rigden, writing in 1987:

> The first law ... is a logician's nightmare. ... To teach Newton's laws so that we prompt no questions of substance is to be unfaithful to the discipline itself. (Rigden, 1987)

As foreboding as the challenge of making sense of Newton's laws might seem, an honest philosopher of physics must try to make progress here – and, indeed, philosophers have engaged with these questions in a surprisingly diverse range of manners. In my view, in order to appreciate the range of options which are available in answering the aforementioned questions, it is helpful to present two approaches which, in many respects, are polar opposites: the 'dynamics first' approach of Brown (2005), and the 'geometry first' approach of Friedman (1983). Indeed, I will use these two authors (and their respective allies) as poles for navigation not just through this section, but over the course of the entirety of this Element.

1.2 Inertial Frames

I will begin with the fourth question in the preceding list: in which frames of reference are Newton's laws supposed to hold?[3] Focusing on **N1L**, it is transparent that this law cannot hold in *all* frames of reference, for envisage a

---

[3] For the time being, I make no distinction between a frame of reference and a coordinate system. Some authors regard the former as consisting in 'extra structure' – I will return later to this idea of 'extra structure', but here I set it aside. (For more on the difference between frames and coordinate systems, see Earman and Friedman (1973).)

force-free body moving with uniform velocity according to some temporal and spatial coordinates, then move to a coordinate system accelerating with respect to the first. In this new coordinate system, the force-free body no longer moves with uniform velocity! Thus, Newton's laws obtain only in particular frames of reference.

We can make these points quantitative as follows. In a given coordinate system x^μ ($\mu = 0,\ldots,3$),[4] suppose the path of any free particle can be expressed as

$$\frac{d^2 x^\mu}{d\tau^2} = 0, \tag{1}$$

where τ is a monotonic parameter on the path in question. Integration yields

$$x^\mu(\tau) = x^\mu(0) + \tau v^\mu(0), \tag{2}$$

where $v^\mu(0) = \frac{dx^\mu}{d\tau}$ at $\tau = 0$, so we obtain straight-line motion in the four-dimensional manifold. *This* is the property which **N1L** tells us holds of force-free particles – so in the frames in which **N1L** holds, we have $\frac{d^2 x^\mu}{d\tau^2} = 0$.

Now perform an arbitrary coordinate transformation $x^\mu \to x'^\mu(x^\nu)$, along with an arbitrary parameter transformation $\tau \to \lambda(\tau)$. Our simple force law $\frac{d^2 x^\mu}{d\tau^2} = 0$ becomes, in the new frame (Brown, 2005, p. 17),

$$\frac{d^2 x'^\mu}{d\lambda^2} - \frac{\partial^2 x'^\mu}{\partial x^\rho \partial x^\gamma} \frac{\partial x^\rho}{\partial x'^\nu} \frac{\partial x^\gamma}{\partial x'^\sigma} \frac{dx'^\nu}{d\lambda} \frac{dx'^\sigma}{d\lambda} = \frac{d^2 \tau}{d\lambda^2} \frac{d\lambda}{d\tau} \frac{dx'^\mu}{d\lambda}. \tag{3}$$

So force-free particles *accelerate* in arbitrary frames (the acceleration is quantified by the two extra terms which have been introduced in this frame: sometimes, these are called 'fictitious force' terms) – they only move on straight lines in the inertial frames.

It is crucial to note at this point that the frames in which **N1L** holds are those in which the very same dynamics takes a particularly simple form.[5] Recalling our discussion of the calendar systems, let us call the frames of reference in which Newton's laws hold the *inertial frames* of reference. Knox, indeed, gives the following very sensible definition of inertial frames:

> In Newtonian theories, and in special relativity, inertial frames have at least the following three features:

---

[4] It is standard practice in physics to use Greek indices ($\mu, \nu, \ldots$) to range over the four coordinates of space *and* time (where the 0 coordinate is the time coordinate), and to use Latin indices $i, j, \ldots$ to range over the three spatial coordinates. I will follow suit in this Element.

[5] Throughout this Element, by dynamical equations taking their 'simplest form' in some coordinate system, I mean something like those equations exhibiting the fewest number of terms in that coordinate system. Although somewhat vague, this notion of simplicity is perfectly clear in practice. For further discussion, see Read, Brown, and Lehmkuhl (2018); Weatherall (2021).

1. Inertial frames are frames with respect to which force-free bodies move with constant velocities.
2. The laws of physics take the same form (a particularly simple one) in all inertial frames.
3. All bodies and physical laws pick out the same equivalence class of inertial frames (universality). (Knox, 2013, p. 348)

So, Newton's laws hold in the inertial frames of reference, which are those coordinate systems in which the dynamics simplify maximally and in which force-free bodies move with uniform velocities. It is important to note, though, that this definition of an inertial frame is what is known as a *functional* definition: it tells us the properties which we expect (or, indeed, demand) that the objects in question (here, inertial frames) possess, but it does not (as yet) afford us any independent means of identifying those objects (again, here frames), or knowing whether they exist. Indeed, it is exactly at this juncture that authors such as Brown and Friedman begin to follow different courses. Beginning with the existence question, Brown maintains that inertial frames *do* exist in nature:

> A kind of highly non-trivial pre-established harmony is being postulated, and it takes the form of the claim that there exists a coordinate system x^μ and parameters τ such that $[\frac{d^2 x^\mu}{d\tau^2} = 0]$ holds for each and every free particle in the universe. (Brown, 2005, p. 17)

On the other hand, Friedman denies the existence of inertial frames:

> Newtonian physics is (would be) true even if there are (were) no inertial frames. The First Law deals with the existence of inertial frames only counterfactually: if there were inertial frames (for example, if there were no gravitational forces), free particles would satisfy $[\frac{d^2 x^\mu}{d\tau^2} = 0]$ in them. (Friedman, 1983, p. 118)

The difference between our two authors amounts to this. Friedman's point is that no particle is *actually* force-free, so inertial frames in the strict sense do not *actually* exist. Brown, on the other hand, would reply that inertial frames at least *approximately* exist. In fact, though, Friedman anticipates this response on behalf of Brown when he writes:

> This reply is inadequate. Newtonian physics is only approximately true, but not because of the existence of *gravity* [i.e., some universal physical force]. (Friedman, 1983, p. 118)

The reader would be forgiven for finding this passage from Friedman puzzling at this stage. It will make more sense once we understand in more detail the differing theoretical commitments of the parties involved – for this reason, I will defer a detailed discussion of this response until the end of the following subsection. For the time being, we need only note this: for Brown, **N1L** is a claim about the existence of (approximate) inertial frames in the real world; for Friedman, by contrast, **N1L** is a counterfactual statement, since in fact there are no inertial frames in the actual world. So much for the existence question. But the question of what the inertial frames *are* remains. To make progress here, we must turn now to the first of the questions in our list: what is the meaning of 'force-free'?

1.3 Force-Free Bodies

To get a better handle on what it means for a particle to be force-free, we must turn to **N2L**, which (recall) says that the total force on a body is equal to the product of that body's (inertial) mass and its acceleration. With **N2L** in mind, a natural further conceptual puzzle arises: is not **N1L** just a special case of **N2L**, given that the former (it seems) reduces to the latter in the case $\mathbf{F} = 0$? Friedman straightforwardly gives an affirmative answer to this question. On the other hand, Brown gives a negative answer:

> It will be recalled that the acceleration $\ddot{x}$ of the body is defined relative to the inertial frame arising out of the first law of motion. It is for this reason that the first law is not a special case of the second for $\mathbf{F} = 0$. (Brown, 2005, p. 37, fn. 9)

In other words, for Brown, **N1L** plays the crucial role of telling us *what the inertial frames are*; for this reason, and in this sense, **N1L** is not merely a special case of **N2L**. I will come back to this, but before doing so let me explain why Friedman *does* think that **N2L** is a special case of **N1L**.

For Friedman, notions of acceleration and force are to be defined in terms of a background spatio-temporal structure. (For the time being, I will not address the question of the metaphysical status of this spatio-temporal structure, and its relation to material bodies – that is, I will not address the substantival-ism/relationalism debate (on which see Pooley, 2013); I will have more to say on this in later sections, in particular Section 7.) In Newtonian mechanics, for Friedman, a particle is genuinely accelerating just in case it follows a curved path with respect to the standard of straightness of paths across time given by (neo-)Newtonian spacetime.[6] A particle is force-free just in case it follows a straight path with respect to that standard of straightness.[7] This gives us a

---

[6] I will explain the 'neo-' prefix here, as well as the general notion of spacetime in Newtonian mechanics, in Section 5 and 6.

[7] More on what this standard of straightness amounts to in Sections 5 and 6.

definition of force-freeness *and* makes clear that **N1L** is just a special case of **N2L**. Thus, helping oneself to a background spatio-temporal structure as does Friedman affords elegant and simple answers to the questions of what it means for a body to genuinely accelerate and what it means for a particle to be force-free. Indeed, this approach also affords a very straightforward independent definition of an inertial frame: the inertial frames are those at rest or moving uniformly *with respect to Newtonian absolute space.*[8]

Brown rejects Friedman's spacetime-based answers to these questions, for in his view such explanations are either opaque (what exactly is the relation between spacetime structure and the motions of material bodies?) or not explanations at all (if spacetime – as is the case for Brown, as we will see – is to be reduced to the motions of material bodies and the dynamical laws governing them, then ultimately I need a way of understanding notions of, for example, force-freeness with reference to material bodies only). In a sense, Brown's philosophical attitude is more *empiricist* than that of Friedman: he seeks an understanding of the notion of an inertial frame (say) directly in terms of material entities, rather than in terms of the (for him) more ethereal notion of spacetime. In fact, there is a long tradition, going back to Lange, Thomson, Tait, and others, of attempting to *empirically ground* the notions of inertial motion, force-freeness, and so forth (Barbour, 1989, ch. 12); Brown certainly can be situated as an ally of this tradition.

There are, indeed, a few different ways in which one might seek to define notions of force-freeness and so forth in an empiricist manner. The approach Brown favours is to take force-free bodies to be those which are sufficiently isolated from all other bodies in the universe; one *defines* such bodies to be force-free and defines inertial frames as those in which such bodies move with uniform velocities (recalling the quote from Brown, we can now see why the fact that a single frame exists in which all such bodies move with uniform velocities is '[a] kind of highly non-trivial pre-established harmony' (Brown, 2005, pp. 16–17)). Brown takes **N1L** to offer this prescription implicitly; any particle accelerating in such a frame is then regarded as subject to a genuine force, as per **N2L**. Note that, if such an approach is successful, no appeal to spacetime structure was needed to afford meaning to the relevant terms under consideration.

Brown's own preferred approach is, however, not the only means by which one might seek an empiricist grounding of the notions of inertial frame,

---

[8] I do not mean to suggest this definition is devoid of problems: open questions remain regarding why such frames are those in which the motions of *material* bodies should simplify maximally. I will return to this issue in later sections.

force-freeness, and so forth. Another option is found in what is known as the 'regularity relationalism' of Huggett (2006). I do not need to get into the details of this view here; rather, a sanitised presentation of the prescription will suffice:[9]

1. Find the frame in which the dynamical equations governing the greatest number of bodies simplify across the total history of the universe.
2. By definition, these are the inertial frames.
3. Any body which follows a straight trajectory in these frames is force-free, by definition.
4. (It is a *conspiracy* – the *conspiracy of inertia* – that these force-free bodies all follow straight-line trajectories in these frames.)
5. Any body which does *not* follow a straight-line trajectory in these frames is subject to a genuine force.
6. **N1L** is not a special case of **N2L** because the accelerations in the latter are with respect to the inertial structure picked out in the former.
7. Extra forces in non-inertial frames are classified as 'fictitious'.

What are the merits of the 'Brown-style' prescription over the 'Huggett-style' prescription, or vice versa? One advantage of the latter is that it makes no initial assumption about the nature of forces in the universe – by contrast, Brown assumes that forces fall off with distances. On the other hand, Huggett's approach assumes that one must have a 'God's-eye view' of the entire material content of the universe – Brown, by contrast, does not do this.

For my purposes, it does not matter which of these approaches one prefers. (To anticipate, there are also other empiricist approaches to the meaning of 'force-free': for example, Torretti (1983) seeks to identify the inertial frames with those frames of reference in which **N3L** holds: I will get back to this shortly.) The central point is that none of these approaches (seem to) require recourse to spatio-temporal structure in order to afford meaning to the terms under consideration.

> **Question:** Which empiricist approach to the content of Newton's laws do you think is superior, and why?

Having now better understood the differences between Brown and Friedman with respect to the notions of inertial frames and force-free bodies, return now to the quote from Friedman presented at the end of the previous subsection.

---

[9] I should be clear that the following is only *inspired* by Huggett's work; I do not mean to claim he would actually endorse it.

This, I claim, is best understood as follows. Friedman supposes initially that Newton's laws are true, where the relevant terms are to be cashed out in terms of the structure of (neo-)Newtonian spacetime, as we have already seen. He also supposes material bodies interact with one another via the gravitational force. In a universe of sufficient complexity (such as the actual world, at least when appropriately idealised), the nature of the gravitational interaction will mean *no* body is truly force-free, in the sense of moving on a uniform trajectory with respect to the standard of straightness given by the background spacetime. For Friedman, the nature of the gravitational force does not mean Newtonian mechanics is in fact false (which would render the theory, in a certain sense, self-undermining), but rather that there simply are no inertial frames embodied as the rest frames of observers in the actual world.

Brown's perspective is very different: he does *not* begin by countenancing entire universes in which such-and-such laws (in this case, Newtonian gravity) obtain; rather, his concern is to afford meaning to notions and certain terms (in this case, for example, 'inertial frame') such that one may then proceed to *build up* one's theoretical commitments. For Brown, a definition of inertial frames (say) which obtains only approximately is still sufficient to build up, in a useful way, the machinery of Newton's laws. In this sense, while Friedman's critique makes sense in the context of his own theoretical commitments, it misfires against the very different methodology of Brown, who has not even constructed the notion of the gravitational interaction at the point when he seeks to define an operationalised notion of inertial frames.

There are various ways of putting the differences between the two parties here. For 'geometrical' authors such as Friedman, it is quite common to take a 'transcendent' conception of physics (in the Kantian sense of 'stepping outside of the world'), and to account for physical phenomena from that perspective, with all of the metaphysics it entails (in particular, the metaphysics of particular physical theories, e.g., Newtonian gravity) as inputs. For 'dynamical' authors such as Brown, by contrast, it is more common to take an 'immanent' conception of physics (in the Kantian sense of being 'embedded in the world'), and to construct the relevant metaphysical and physical notions on the basis of empirical studies in the world. This is vague, but I think useful to keep in mind when one reads debates between the relevant authors: failure to keep track of these different attitudes can often lead to individuals talking past one another, as the passage from Friedman indicates.[10]

---

[10] When put in this way, it is not completely obvious that the two views are incompatible: one begins with empirical data, 'ascends' (via the 'dynamical' approach) to a set of metaphysical commitments, which one then uses to 'descend' (via the 'geometrical' approach) to explain

Question: Do you think Brown's 'dynamics first' approach to the content of Newton's laws is to be preferred over Friedman's 'geometry first' approach, or vice versa? Why?

1.4 Summary of the Views

Let us return to our list of conceptual questions regarding Newton's laws, and consider how both Brown and Friedman would answer these questions. (For the time being, I omit the fifth question; I will discuss that in the following subsection.) First Brown:

1. Bodies are to be designated 'force-free' on the basis of some to-be-articulated operational procedure.
2. **N1L** is not a case of **N2L** because **N1L** allows us to identify the inertial frames (those in which force-free bodies move with uniform velocities); having fixed such frames, **N2L** then allows us to identify the particles subject to genuine forces (and the magnitudes of those forces).
3. **N1L** is not a definition – force-free particles are not *defined* to be those moving with uniform velocity.
4. Newton's laws are supposed to hold in the inertial frames of reference.

As we know by now, the answers Friedman would give to these four questions are very different:

1. 'Force-free' means moving uniformly with respect to the standard of straightness given by (neo-)Newtonian spacetime.
2. **N1L** is a special case of **N2L**.
3. **N1L** is not a definition – in fact, it is redundant.
4. As stated in a coordinate-based description, Newton's laws are supposed to hold in the inertial frames, which are the frames 'adapted' to (neo-)Newtonian spacetime (i.e., are the frames at rest or moving uniformly with respect to Newtonian absolute spacetime). Insofar as a world (e.g., an idealised version of the actual world) may in fact contain no bodies which are truly force-free, **N1L** cannot be operationalised in that world (in this sense, **N1L** obtains only counterfactually).

The reader will notice that, up to this point, I have not mentioned **N3L**, and I have not addressed the associated question (5), of whether **N1L** is a special

---

further data. This tale of ascent and descent is a familiar one in philosophy, going back to Plato's cave. (My thanks to Niels Linnemann for discussions here.)

case of **N3L**. This is the final piece of the puzzle regarding Newton's laws; I turn now to this issue.

1.5 Newton's Third Law

What is the conceptual relation between **N3L** and **N1L** and **N2L**? One of the few authors to address this question in any detail is Torretti, who writes:

> [T]he Third Law of Motion furnishes a Newtonian physicist with all he needs for distinguishing, in principle, between a particle acted on by a true force of nature and a free particle accelerating in a particular – necessarily non-inertial – frame. If a material particle α of mass m experiences acceleration a in an inertial frame F, it will instantaneously react with force $-m$a on the material source of its acceleration. There must exist therefore a material system β, of mass m/k, whose centre of mass experiences in F the acceleration $-k$a. On the other hand, if a particle α accelerates in a non-inertial frame, its acceleration must include a component that is not matched by the acceleration of another material system, in direction opposite to the said component, caused by the action of α on that system. (Torretti, 1983, pp. 19–20)

Torretti continues in an endnote:

> The criterion furnished by the Third Law does not, of course, amount to an 'operational definition' of a *freely moving particle* and an *inertial frame*. In the above example, the acceleration of β by α's reaction will generally be only a component of β's total acceleration and it might not be easy to discern it. But the criterion surely bestows a definite, intelligible meaning on the italicised expressions. (Torretti, 1983, p. 287, n. 16)

Torretti's claim here is that a frame in which **N1L** is satisfied is one in which **N3L** is satisfied, and vice versa. Moreover, one can thereby in principle – if not in practice – check whether **N3L** is satisfied in a given frame, and (if so) use this fact to identify operationally/empirically the force-free bodies (thus, this constitutes a third approach to the operational identification of force-free particles, alongside the Brown-style and Huggett-style approaches discussed earlier).

Let us focus first on the claim that **N1L** implies **N3L** – equivalently, that **N3L** is presupposed by **N1L**. At least in the context of special relativity, this claim is not correct, for, as Griffiths writes,

> Unlike the first two, Newton's *third* law does not, in general, extend to the relativistic domain. Indeed, if the two objects in question are separated in space, the third law is incompatible with the relativity of simultaneity. For suppose the force of A on B at some instant t is $F(t)$, and the force of B on A at the same instant is $-F(t)$; then the third law applies *in this reference*

frame. But a moving observer will report that these equal and opposite forces occurred at *different times*; in his system, therefore, the third law is violated. Only in the case of contact interactions, where the two forces are applied at the same physical point (and in the trivial case where the forces are constant) can the third law be retained. (Griffiths, 2013, p. 544)

Although Griffiths puts the point in terms of an incompatibility between **N3L** and the relativity of simultaneity (see Section 8), the fundamental tension is between **N3L** and the relativity *principle* (see Section 2): in cases such as this example, in which the forces between the bodies in question (in that example, α and β) are not mediated by contact interactions, if **N3L** holds in one frame of reference F, then it will not hold in a frame F' in uniform motion with respect to F – that is, **N3L** will not hold in another inertial frame of reference, in violation of the relativity principle.

In response to this, one might reasonably complain that, at least within the context of Newtonian forces, there is no reason to doubt this claim. Moreover, recall from the foregoing discussion that the point of the 'dynamics first', more 'operational' outlook of authors such as Brown was to build up one's theoretical commitments on the basis of empirical data, without making theoretical assumptions *ab initio*. Therefore, to appeal to relativity theory may be to make a *petitio principii* against such authors, who could simply *define* the force-free bodies to be those moving on uniform trajectories in the **N3L**-satisfying frames.

In any case, let us turn now to the other professed direction of implication – that **N3L** implies **N1L** – equivalently, that **N1L** is presupposed by **N3L**. Here, there seem to be counterexamples coming from within the context of Newtonian mechanics. For example, consider a Newtonian universe consisting of one single binary astronomical system, in which two bodies α and β of equal mass rotate about a common centre of mass. Consider a frame rotating about said centre of mass: the force on α will be equal and opposite to the force on β – in spite of the fact that these two bodies will be subject to (equal and opposite) inertial effects. This frame is non-inertial, but **N3L** is satisfied. Thus, any claim that the satisfaction of **N3L** implies that the system in question is being described in an inertial frame of reference is incorrect; rather, the inertial systems are (at best) a *subclass* of the **N3L**-satisfying systems.

Examples like this seem to imply that one cannot *invariably* use **N3L** as a means of operationally identifying the inertial frames – indeed, one can make this point without having to worry about the reverse direction of implication. As before, however, it is not obvious that these concerns need animate those who situate themselves in the 'dynamical' camp.

> **Question:** How general and how serious are problem cases of the kind introduced in this subsection? In light of this, to what extent can something of Torretti's claim be salvaged?

1.6 Summary

I do not deny that this has been a difficult first section. But, by proceeding from Newton's laws, I hope to have illustrated that one encounters deep, profound, and unresolved questions in the foundations of spacetime theories from the very outset. Proceeding in this way also has the merit of introducing at the beginning a number of crucial concepts which will animate us over the course of the remainder of this Element: concepts such as inertial frames, force-free motion, and dynamical versus geometrical understandings of physics. I will, indeed, return to all of these issues in the context of special relativity quite shortly. Before doing so, however, it is necessary to introduce some further concepts – in particular, the concept of a *symmetry* of a physical theory. I turn to this task in the next section.

2 Symmetries and Invariance

My goals in this section are threefold: (i) to introduce the notion of a *symmetry* of a physical theory, (ii) to explore how such symmetries might be identified, and (iii) to convince the reader of the significance of symmetry-based reasoning in physics.

2.1 The Relativity Principle

Suppose you decide to take the sleeper train from Euston to Fort William; outside, it is pitch black – you cannot see a thing. Ignoring the mild jostling from side to side which inevitably one experiences on a train, can you tell the speed at which your train is moving? If the train is moving uniformly at 100 mph, is there any empirical difference inside the train to the situation in which it is at rest? The answer, of course, is *no* – and this is one illustration of what is known as the *relativity principle*: for a subsystem appropriately isolated from the environment, the laws of physics inside the system are exactly the same, whatever the uniform velocity of that system might be.[11]

---

[11] Galileo was one of the first to present the relativity principle in this form, and his presentation remains one of the most elegant: see Galilei (1967, pp. 186–7).

We saw in the previous section that the inertial frames are those frames in which the dynamical equations governing matter take their simplest form, and in which force-free bodies move with uniform velocity. When this is combined with the relativity principle, we arrive at the conclusion that the laws of physics take their simplest in all of a *class* of inertial frames, which are related by uniform velocity transformations. But what exactly are these 'uniform velocity transformations' in Newtonian mechanics, and are they the same transformations which take us between inertial frames in special relativity? (Spoiler: no!) To answer the first question, we need to investigate the invariance properties of Newtonian theories. Before doing so, however, there is one other important conceptual distinction to clear up: that between active and passive transformations.

2.2 Active versus Passive Transformations

There is an important distinction between *active* and *passive* transformations, the prescriptions for which can be put as follows:

Active transformations: Transform physical system; leave coordinate system unchanged.
Passive transformations: Transform coordinate system; leave physical system unchanged.

The transformations considered in this section can be understood either actively or passively; more generally, over the course of this Element, I will be explicit about whether a transformation is active or passive. Although mathematically active and passive transformations have the same net result, conceptually they are clearly very different; these differences have turned out to have quite serious ramifications for various debates in the foundations of spacetime theories.[12]

With the distinction between active and passive transformations in hand, we are in a better position to understand what is going on in the case of Galileo's ship (or, equivalently, our original train example). Suppose we apply an active transformation to a subsystem of the universe. Then, assuming

1. the relativity principle holds, and
2. the subsystem is *isolated* from that of the environment,

---

[12] The most (in)famous example is the 'hole argument' of general relativity – see, for example, Norton (2022) and Pooley (2021).

the physics within the subsystem will be unchanged between the pre- and post-transformed cases. This – an active boost applied to a subsystem, assuming the relativity principle and dynamical isolation – is what is going on in Galileo's ship.

2.3 Galilean Transformations

Let us now return to the main project in this section: to introduce and provide some means of ascertaining the symmetries of Newtonian physical theories. For Newtonian theories, I will begin by giving the game away: their symmetries at least include (but do not necessarily exhaust: this will be of significance later) the Galilean transformations. A *Galilean transformation* is any coordinate transformation that can be expressed as the composition of a rigid spacetime translation, a rigid rotation, and a Galilean boost:

Spatial translation	g_a $(a \in \mathbb{R}^3)$:	$g_a(t, \mathbf{x}) = (t, \mathbf{x} + \mathbf{a})$.
Time translation	g_b $(b \in \mathbb{R})$:	$g_b(t, \mathbf{x}) = (t + b, \mathbf{x})$.
Spatial rotation	g_R $(\mathbf{R} \in SO\,(3))$:	$g_R(t, \mathbf{x}) = (t, \mathbf{Rx})$.
Galilean boost	g_v $(\mathbf{v} \in \mathbb{R}^3)$:	$g_v(t, \mathbf{x}) = (t, \mathbf{x} - \mathbf{v}t)$.

How do I show that a given set of physical laws has (say) the Galilean transformations as its symmetries? There are two ways of defining what it means for a given set of laws to be invariant under a given set of transformations: the 'space-of-solutions approach' and the 'form-of-equations approach'. I will illustrate both, beginning with the space-of-solutions approach.

Consider the equation of motion

$$\frac{dr}{dt} = -kr. \tag{4}$$

This has general solution

$$r(t) = Ae^{-kt}, \qquad A \in \mathbb{R}. \tag{5}$$

For any such r and any time translation g_b, we can form the transformed structure $g_b r$:

$$
\begin{aligned}
(g_b r)(t) &= r(t - b) \\
&= Ae^{-k(t-b)} \\
&= \left(Ae^{+kb}\right)e^{-kt}.
\end{aligned}
\tag{6}
$$

This is another solution of the same equation, so we say our equation is *time-translation invariant*.

More generally, the space-of-solutions approach takes the following form:

Space-of-Solutions Approach

1. Identify the set Θ of equations to be investigated.
2. Identify a set S of *structures for* Θ – that is, identify the type of object that is mathematically appropriate to be a candidate *solution* to Θ.
3. Identify the group G of transformations whose effects on Θ we will be interested in investigating.
4. For general $g \in G$, identify the action of g on S.
5. Ask whether this action of G preserves the subset $D \subset S$ of solutions to Θ.

It is also worth considering the case of a demonstration of *non*-invariance on the space-of-solutions approach. Let the equation of motion (and hence Θ and S) be as before. Let G be the group B_1 of one-dimensional *boosts* $g_v : x \mapsto x - vt$. The action of any such g_v on S is:

$$(g_v r)(t) = r(t) - vt. \tag{7}$$

For the general solution $r(t) = Ae^{-kt}$, the transformed structure is given by

$$(g_v r)(t) = Ae^{-kt} - vt, \tag{8}$$

which is *not* identical to Be^{-kt} for any $B \in \mathbb{R}$ – that is, is not a solution of our original equation. So our equation is not *Galilean boost invariant*.

So much for the space-of-solutions approach; let us turn now to the form-of-equations approach. Consider again the equation of motion (4). This equation is built from various objects: $\frac{d}{dt}$, r, and k. Under a time-translation g_b,

- $\frac{d}{dt}$ and k transform trivially;
- the function r transforms, as before, as $(g_b r)(t) = r(t - b)$.

The transformed equation is therefore

$$\frac{d}{dt} r(t - b) = -kr(t - b). \tag{9}$$

But asserting that our second equation holds for all t is equivalent to asserting that our first equation holds for all t. Thus, the original equation is time translation invariant.

The general format of the form-of-equations approach is this:

Form-of-Equations Approach

1. Identify the set of equations Θ to be investigated.
2. Identify the group G of transformations whose effects on Θ we will be interested in investigating.
3. Identify an action of G on each of the ingredients in each equation in Θ.
4. Write down the equations with the transformed ('primed') quantities in place of the untransformed ones.
5. If the result is a set of equations equivalent to the original Θ, then Θ is G-invariant.

And here is a demonstration of non-invariance of an equation on the form-of-equations approach. Consider once again the equation of motion (4). Let G be the group B_1 of one-dimensional boosts $g_v : x \mapsto x - vt$. The ingredients of our equation transform as

$$g_v : \frac{d}{dt} \mapsto \frac{d}{dt}; \tag{10}$$

$$g_v : k \mapsto k; \tag{11}$$

$$g_v : r(t) \mapsto r(t) - vt. \tag{12}$$

So the transformed equation is

$$\frac{d}{dt}(r(t) - vt) = -k(r(t) - vt). \tag{13}$$

But this is equivalent to the original equation only if $-v = vkt$, which clearly cannot hold for all t. The *non*-equivalence of the untransformed and transformed equations means the original equation is *not* boost-invariant.

Although I earlier used a very simple toy model, it is straightforward to apply both of these approaches to more physically relevant theories. A standard first-year presentation of Newtonian gravity for two particles is given by (combining N2L and the law of gravitation):

$$\ddot{\mathbf{r}}_i = \frac{G_N m_1 m_2}{|\mathbf{r}_1 - \mathbf{r}_2|^3}(\mathbf{r}_i - \mathbf{r}_{i+1}), \qquad i = 1, 2. \tag{14}$$

Let G be the group B_3 of *three*-dimensional boosts, $\{(g_{\mathbf{v}} : \mathbf{r} \mapsto \mathbf{r} - \mathbf{v}t) : \mathbf{v} \in \mathbb{R}^3\}$. The quantities in our equation transform as

$$\mathbf{r}'_i(t) := (g_{\mathbf{v}}\mathbf{r}_i)(t) = \mathbf{r}_i(t) - \mathbf{v}t, \tag{15}$$

$$\ddot{\mathbf{r}}'_i(t) := (g_{\mathbf{v}}\ddot{\mathbf{r}}_i)(t) = \ddot{\mathbf{r}}_i(t), \tag{16}$$

$$m_i' := g_{\mathbf{v}} m_i = m_i.\tag{17}$$

The transformed equation is:

$$\ddot{\mathbf{r}}_i' = \frac{G_N m_1 m_2}{\left|\mathbf{r}_1' - \mathbf{r}_2'\right|^3}\left(\mathbf{r}_i' - \mathbf{r}_{i+1}'\right), \qquad i = 1, 2.\tag{18}$$

Eliminating the primes, we have

$$\ddot{\mathbf{r}}_i = \frac{G_N m_1 m_2}{\left|\mathbf{r}_1 - \mathbf{r}_2\right|^3}\left(\mathbf{r}_i - \mathbf{r}_{i+1}\right), \qquad i = 1, 2.\tag{19}$$

So the equation (14) is form-invariant under Galilean boosts!

Exercise: Generalise this to the N-body problem.

Exercise: Show that Newtonian gravitation is invariant under Galilean boosts using the space-of-solutions approach.

Having now presented both methods for ascertaining whether a given set of equations has a given set of symmetries, there are a couple of conceptual points to make. First: pragmatically, there is some reason to prefer the form-of-equations approach over the space-of-solutions approach because the former does not involve having to figure out what the solutions of the equation under consideration *actually are*. Second: in each case, we began with an *ansatz* about the symmetry group of our equation. Figuring out the full symmetry group of a set of equations is highly non-trivial. While there is no general method for doing this, the task can be aided by formulating our theories in certain ways, using certain objects which have familiar symmetry properties. (I will demonstrate explicitly what I mean by this in Section 6.)

Question: Are the space-of-solutions approach and the form-of-equations approach equivalent?

2.4 Newton on Galilean Invariance

I am now going to indulge in an historical digression. Newton claims to infer Galilean invariance from his laws of motion: after setting out the latter, he infers several corollaries; his 'Corollary V' is:

> The motions of bodies included in a given space are the same among themselves, whether that space is at rest, or moves uniformly forward in a right line without any circular motion. (Cajori, 1934, p. 20)

This essentially *states* that the laws of physics are Galilean invariant. Newton's argument for Corollary V is this:

> For the differences of the motions tending towards the same parts, and the sums of those that tend toward contrary parts, are, at first (by supposition), in both cases the same; and it is from those sums and differences that the collisions and impulses do arise with which the bodies mutually impinge one upon another. Wherefore (by Law II) the effects of those collisions will be equal in both cases; and therefore the mutual motions of the bodies among themselves in the one case will remain equal to the mutual motions of the bodies among themselves in the other. A clear proof of which we have from experiment of a ship; where all motions happen after the same manner, whether the ship is at rest, or is carried uniformly forwards in a right line. (Cajori, 1934, p. 20)

Newton's reasoning here is morally correct, but it is worth pointing to a couple of non sequiturs in his argument. First: it does not follow from the laws of motion alone that 'it is from those sums and differences that the collisions and impulses do arise with which the bodies mutually impinge upon one another'. This requires the *additional assumption* that forces depend only on (vectorial) differences of positions and/or velocities, not on absolute positions or absolute velocities. (Consider a particle affected by the force $\mathbf{F} = -k\mathbf{v}$.) Second: it does not follow that 'the effects of those collisions will be equal' unless we further assume that the *mass* of a given body is independent of the body's absolute position and absolute velocity. (Consider particles whose masses are proportional to their absolute speeds.) That said, with these two auxiliary assumptions in place, Galilean invariance of the laws does follow from **N2L** (by essentially Newton's argument). (For more on this, see (Brown, 2005, §3.2).)

2.5 Poincaré Transformations

So far, I have introduced the Galilean transformations, as well as two different methods for checking whether a given set of equations has a given set of transformations as symmetries. Of course, though, the Galilean transformations are not the only set of transformations of physical interest – and, indeed (to anticipate), the transformations which are most relevant to special relativity are the *Poincaré transformations*. We saw that a Galilean transformation can be expressed as the composition of a rigid spacetime translation, a rigid rotation, and a Galilean boost. A *Poincaré transformation* is any coordinate transformation that can be expressed as the composition of a rigid spacetime translation, a rigid rotation, and a *Lorentz* boost:[13]

---

[13] Here, I use the Einstein summation convention, according to which repeated indices in a term are summed. I also use four-dimensional index notation, which will be discussed in detail in Section 6.

Spacetime translation $g_{a^\mu}\left(a^\mu \in \mathbb{R}^4\right):$ $g_{a^\mu}(x^\nu) = x^\nu + a^\nu.$

Spatial rotation and Lorentz boost $g_{\Lambda^\mu{}_\nu}\left(\Lambda^\mu{}_\nu \in SO(1,3)\right):$ $g_{\Lambda^\mu{}_\nu}(x^\nu) = \Lambda^\nu{}_\sigma x^\sigma.$

In both cases, we have a rigid translation, a rigid rotation, and a boost. But the boosts are *different* in the two cases. To render this explicit: here is a Galilean boost in the x direction:

$$t' = t, \tag{20}$$

$$x' = x - vt. \tag{21}$$

By contrast, here is a Lorentz boost in the x direction ($\gamma := 1/\sqrt{1 - v^2/c^2}$):

$$t' = \gamma\left(t - \frac{vx}{c^2}\right), \tag{22}$$

$$x' = \gamma(x - vt). \tag{23}$$

Question: Is there any reason to prefer $c \to \infty$ or $v/c \to 0$ as a way of taking the non-relativistic limit of the Lorentz transformations? What additional assumptions does one need to make in order to recover the Galilean boosts from the Lorentz boosts when $v/c \to 0$?

The first set of physical laws which were discovered to be Poincaré invariant were Maxwell's equations. In their typical three-vector formulation, these read:[14]

$$\nabla \cdot \mathbf{E} = \rho, \tag{24}$$

$$\nabla \cdot \mathbf{B} = 0, \tag{25}$$

$$\nabla \times \mathbf{E} = -\frac{\partial \mathbf{B}}{\partial t}, \tag{26}$$

$$\nabla \times \mathbf{B} = \mathbf{J} + \frac{\partial \mathbf{E}}{\partial t}. \tag{27}$$

Maxwell's equations are invariant under Poincaré transformations; they are not invariant under Galilean transformations. One might indeed say it was the discovery of a set of dynamical laws which were Poincaré invariant rather than Galilean invariant which precipitated the crisis in nineteenth-century physics which eventually led to the development of special relativity. It is this crisis I am going to discuss in the next section.

---

[14] Note that changing just one sign in Maxwell's equations will change their symmetry properties: see Heras (1994).

3 The Michelson–Morley Experiment

I intimated at the end of the previous section that the discovery of Maxwell's equations – which are invariant under Poincaré transformations – precipitated a crisis in nineteenth-century physics. Here is a quick and dirty way to see the issue, in terms of symmetries.[15] We have seen that Newtonian mechanics is invariant under Galilean transformations – that is, translations, spatial rotations, and Galilean boosts. We have also seen that electromagnetism is invariant under Poincaré transformations – that is, translations, spatial rotations, and Lorentz boosts. Suppose we lived in a world in which both of these theories were true. Then the overall invariance group of the physical laws of the world would be the intersection of these two groups – that is, the group of translations and spatial rotations (no boosts). The lack of boost invariance would then imply (up to translations and spatial rotations) the existence of a preferred frame! So in the wake of Maxwell's electromagnetism in the nineteenth century, physicists anticipated violations of the relativity principle.[16]

What did people take the significance of this predicted preferred frame to be? From Maxwell's equations, one can derive that the speed of light is c (see, e.g., Jackson, 1998). It is natural to identify this statement as holding true in the aforementioned preferred frame. In this frame, with respect to what is light moving? The nineteenth-century answer is some background structure: *the ether*, which was supposed to be the medium in which light waves propagate. So (the thought goes) light moves at c in the rest frame of the ether– and this is the preferred frame in which Maxwell's equations hold. This was an extremely sensible thing for nineteenth-century physicists to think, since it rests only on the assumption that light is like all other waves, insofar as (i) it has a medium, and (ii) its speed is independent of the speed of the source (and, insofar as one takes the wave in question to have a medium, a function only of the speed of that medium).[17]

---

[15] This presentation is anachronistic because in fact around the time these events were unfolding in physics (i.e., the 1880s), the symmetry group of Maxwell's equations was yet to be discovered: see Brown (2005, p. 2). Still, the presentation here has the merit of pedagogical clarity.

[16] To repeat the point of the previous footnote: physicists arrived at this conclusion on the basis of the wave-like nature of light (more on which below), rather than on the basis of consideration of symmetry groups. Nevertheless, the central conclusion – the existence of a preferred frame – is the same on either account.

[17] Sometimes, when one first encounters special relativity, (ii) is marketed as a novel feature of light. But this is badly confused, since it is a feature of all waves. As we will see, the distinctive feature of light has to do with the nature of its medium (specifically, it has to do with the fact that we no longer believe the medium exists!).

That light moves at c only in the rest frame of the ether, and moves at $c \pm v$ in a frame moving at velocity v with respect to the ether (because, from Maxwell's equations, the speed of light is independent of the speed of the source – to repeat, the situation here is *exactly the same as for all other waves*[18]), is an *empirical hypothesis* which should be testable. In the nineteenth century, physicists indeed did attempt to test this hypothesis – all tests ended in *null results*. The most famous of these experiments is the *Michelson–Morley experiment*, which I will consider in detail in this section.

3.1 The Michelson–Morley Experiment

How did physicists attempt to test these predictions? By far the most famous such attempted experimental test was the Michelson–Morley experiment.[19] As we have already discussed, assuming that the Earth is moving with some velocity with respect to the ether, there should (the thought went) be differences in the observed velocity of light, which should be detectable. It was exactly these differences which the Michelson–Morley experiment was designed to detect. In Figure 2, I have drawn a schematic representation of the set-up of this experiment, which was designed to work as follows:

1. The interferometer sends a beam of coherent light from a source towards a half-silvered mirror.
2. Here the beam is split into two components that continue at right angles to one another: one down 'arm A' and the other down 'arm B'.
3. A short distance later, each half-beam encounters a second (fully silvered) mirror and is reflected back. The beams are recombined, and the resulting interference pattern is observed on a detector screen.
4. The observed pattern will depend on:
    (a) the lengths of arms A and B, and
    (b) *the speed of travel of the light along each arm in each direction.*

In a lab that is moving relative to the ether with speed v, the speed of light relative to the lab frame is expected to be *anisotropic*: it should be $c - v$ in the direction of the lab's motion, $c + v$ in the opposite direction, and $\sqrt{c^2 - v^2}$

---

[18] Indeed, the wave equation for sound is also invariant under Poincaré transformations – albeit with an invariant speed which is not c, but rather the speed of sound. These parallels raise interesting questions regarding whether (and under what circumstances) one might be led to a relativistic theory on the basis of (say) sound waves, rather than light waves. I will not go into this further here – suffice it to say that exploring the parallels is an illuminating pedagogical exercise. For recent discussions on these matters, see Cheng and Read (2021); Todd and Menicucci (2017); Todd, Pantaleoni, Baccetti, and Menicucci (2021).

[19] For further details, see Brown (2005, ch. 4).

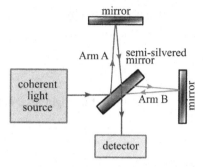

Figure 2 Set-up of the Michelson–Morley experiment

in directions perpendicular to that of the lab's motion (the third velocity can be computed via a straightforward application of Pythagoras' theorem). *If we could ensure that the arms were exactly equal in length, then anything other than constructive interference would indicate the presence of an ether wind.* Unfortunately, ensuring this was not technologically feasible when Michelson and Morley performed their experiment. However, regardless of the arm lengths, *rotating* the apparatus should *change* the interference pattern in a predictable manner in a moving frame, and would not if the apparatus were at rest with respect to the ether. Thus we look for this post-rotation change as a signature of the ether wind.

More quantitatively, the reasoning proceeds as follows. Suppose (for simplicity) that the two arms are of equal length, L. The out-and-back time for light to travel along the arm that is parallel to the ether drift should be

$$\Delta t_{\parallel} = \frac{L}{c-v} + \frac{L}{c+v} = \frac{2Lc}{c^2 - v^2}. \tag{28}$$

The out-and-back time for light to travel along the arm that is *perpendicular* to the ether drift should be

$$\Delta t_{\perp} = \frac{2L}{\sqrt{c^2 - v^2}}. \tag{29}$$

The time difference before rotation is then given by

$$\Delta t_{\parallel} - \Delta t_{\perp} = \frac{2}{c}\left(\frac{L}{1 - \frac{v^2}{c^2}} - \frac{L}{\sqrt{1 - \frac{v^2}{c^2}}} \right). \tag{30}$$

By multiplying by c, the corresponding length difference before rotation is

$$\Delta_1 = 2\left(\frac{L}{1 - \frac{v^2}{c^2}} - \frac{L}{\sqrt{1 - \frac{v^2}{c^2}}} \right). \tag{31}$$

After rotation, the length difference is given by

$$\Delta_2 = 2\left(\frac{L}{\sqrt{1 - \frac{v^2}{c^2}}} - \frac{L}{1 - \frac{v^2}{c^2}}\right). \tag{32}$$

Dividing $\Delta_1 - \Delta_2$ by the wavelength λ of the light used in the interferometer, the fringe shift n is found:

$$n = \frac{\Delta_1 - \Delta_2}{\lambda} \approx \frac{2Lv^2}{\lambda c^2}. \tag{33}$$

If $L = 11m$, $\lambda = 550nm$, and $v = 30kms^{-1}$, this gives an expected fringe shift of $\Delta n \approx 0.4$ – certainly large enough to be observable (*despite* the fact that the effect is second order in v/c).

A couple of comments are helpful at this stage. First, one might wonder: is not a length of $11m$ pretty big for the experiment? Yes – in fact, Michelson and Moreley implemented this *effective* length by using mirrors to bounce light back and forth in their detectors (this method is by now standard, and it is also used in modern interferometers such as LIGO, which was used to detect gravitational waves, as predicted by general relativity). (See Figure 3, from the original paper by Michelson and Morley (1887), in which they illustrate this use of mirrors.) Second, one might wonder: where did the velocity of $30kms^{-1}$ come from? The simple answer is that this was a guess: that velocity is the approximate orbital velocity of the Earth around the Sun, so it seems as good

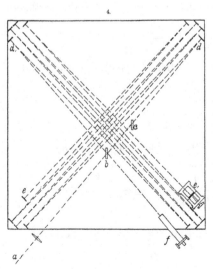

Figure 3 Diagram of the Michelson–Morley experiment (Michelson & Morley, 1887)

as any other from the point of view of rendering quantitative the theoretical predictions regarding this experiment.

In any case, we already know the punchline to this story: The result of the Michelson–Morley experiment was null – rotating the apparatus did not lead to a detectable fringe shift. Michelson and Morley concluded that 'if there be any relative motion between the earth and the luminifeous ether, it must be small' (Michelson & Morley, 1887, p. 341); here, 'small' means 'probably less than one-sixth of the earth's orbital velocity, and certainly less than one-fourth'. This null result was a mystery: this 'small relative motion' might obtain by luck at any given instant, but it is difficult to see how it could obtain *throughout* the Earth's orbit. (Assuming that the ether is an inert background, then *of course* the Earth cannot be at rest with respect to it at every point in its orbit; on the other hand, if the ether is not inert, then it would have to be the case that the Earth (say) drags the ether around its orbit, so that there is no detectable relative motion between the two – but that hypothesis was *ad hoc*; moreover, the drag hypothesis was already losing favour when the Michelson–Morley experiment was performed.[20])

It is worth reiterating the puzzle presented by these null results; we can do so by treating the Earth as in essence an analogue of Galileo's ship. Suppose the Earth is at rest with respect to the ether at some point in its orbit. Then the Earth will be moving with respect to the ether at some other point in its orbit. It will look like the Earth is, therefore, a Galileo ship-type subsystem which has been actively boosted. If all physics were Galilean invariant, we would expect the same physical laws on the Earth in the two scenarios. But electromagnetism is *not* Galilean invariant (it is Poincaré invariant) – so (the thought goes) we should expect violations of the (Galilean) relativity principle manifesting themselves in different detected velocities of light in the two cases. How to explain that this was never observed?

3.2 Lorentz's Programme

It would be easy, through the lens of post-Einsteinian physics, to denigrate the ether theorists as foolish for having chased after a will-o'-the-wisp in the form of the ether. But it bears stressing that there was no reason at the time to doubt the analogies between light and other waves such as sound and water. More-over, as we will see, the work undertaken by physicists such as Fitzgerald, Larmor, and Lorentz in the wake of the Michelson–Moreley null result pro-vided the fuel to ignite Einstein's relativistic revolution. So these physicists

---

[20] For further discussion of this drag hypothesis, see Ryckman (2017, pp. 172–3) and Norton (2018, ch. 8).

have every right to be dubbed, in Brown's words, 'the trailblazers' (Brown, 2005, ch. 4).

Let us begin with Fitzgerald, who in 1889 suggested that 'almost the only hypothesis' capable of reconciling the Michelson-Morley experiment with the apparent fact that the Earth dragged a negligible amount of ether was that

> the length of material bodies changes, according as they are moving through the ether or across it, by an amount depending on the square of the ratio of their velocities to that light. (FitzGerald, 1889)

He continued:

> We know that electric forces are affected by the motion of electrified bodies relative to the ether and it seems a not improbable supposition that the molecular forces are affected by the motion and that the size of the body alters consequently. (FitzGerald, 1889)

The idea here is that we do not observe violations of the relativity principle in the sense of the frame-dependence of the velocity of light, for material bodies contract under velocity boosts in just such a way as to compensate for such effects and yield the recorded null result. Lorentz, indeed, would arrive at the same idea in 1892; Larmor would also adopt the idea in his 1900 book, *Aether and Matter*.

To be a little more concrete (and here I follow the presentation of Brown (2005, §4.4)), Lorentz introduced a longditudinal factor, $C_{\parallel} = 1 + \delta$, and a transverse factor, $C_{\perp} = 1 + \epsilon$. He claimed the null result required

$$\epsilon - \delta \sim \frac{v^2}{2c^2}. \tag{34}$$

Contraction in this manner would cancel out the different velocities of light and lead to no phase shift effects at the detector. Lorentz would later push this idea further with his 'theorem of corresponding states' (Lorentz, 1895). This was designed to show that *no* first- or second-order ether-wind effects would be discernible in experiments involving optics and electrodynamics. In the second version of this theorem, the Lorentz transformations finally appear; however, until Einstein's work in 1905 (see Section 4), Lorentz continued to believe that the true coordinate transformations were the Galilean ones and that these new transformations were merely a useful formal device.

In sum, the reasoning of the ether theorists can be laid out as follows:

1. When I consider the Earth at rest versus moving with some velocity v, I am to construe those states as related by Galilean transformations.

2. Since Maxwell's equations are *not* invariant under such transformations, I should expect different electromagnetic physics in the two states – in particular, I should expect a different velocity of light in the pre- and post-transformed states.
3. In light of the null results of experiments such as that of Michelson and Morley, I postulate that material bodies contract under Galilean boosts – that is, I postulate more relativity principle–violating physics to cancel out the first relativity principle–violating physics and explain why I do not *observe* violations of the relativity principle.

Einstein would reject (1) – I will tackle in detail how he achieved this in the following section, but in brief for now: he would argue that when I consider the Earth at rest versus moving with some velocity v, I am (in light of the dynamical constitution of the bodies under consideration) to construe those states as related by Lorentz transformations, so that (a) the speed of light does not vary from inertial frame to inertial frame, and (b) accordingly, no *ad hoc* compensating dynamical effects are required in order to save the relativity principle.[21]

Continuing to focus on the ether theorists' dynamical contraction hypotheses, I wish to make one further point here. As time went on, the exact nature of dynamical contraction required to underwrite the null results of Michelson–Morely-type experiments became increasingly *ad hoc*. As Brown writes,

> Lorentz noted that the theorem of corresponding states actually implies that the frequency of oscillating electrons in the light source is affected by motion of the source, and it is this fact that gives rise to the change in frequency of the emitted light. But Lorentz realized that the oscillating electrons only satisfy Newton's laws of motion if it is assumed that both their masses and the forces impressed on them depend on the electrons' velocity relative to the ether. The hypotheses in Lorentz's system were starting to pile up, and the spectre of *ad hoc*ness was increasingly hard to ignore (as Poincaré would complain). (Brown, 2005, p. 56)

Something had to give – enter Einstein.

---

[21] Of course, the Lorentz transformations famously entail the phenomenon of length contraction, which will be discussed in detail in Section 9, but for the time being we should take this to have a different conceptual status to the kind of contraction postulated by authors such as Fitzgerald, Larmor, and Lorentz – in effect, Einstein elevated contraction to a *kinematical* effect.

4 Einstein's 1905 Derivation

In 1905, Einstein published four papers in the journal *Annalen der Physik*, each of which precipitated a revolution in physics. The papers were on:

1. The photoelectric effect. (Einstein, 1905c)
2. Brownian motion. (Einstein, 1905b)
3. Special relativity. (Einstein, 1905d)
4. Mass–energy equivalence. (Einstein, 1905a)

Quite rightly, the year would come to be known as Einstein's *annus mirabilis*. Einstein's 1905 derivation of the Lorentz transformations in his third *annus mirabilis* paper, 'On the Electrodynamics of Moving Bodies', purports to account for all null ether wind experiment results, without recourse to dynamical considerations *à la* Lorentz *et al*. In effect, it elevates contraction from a dynamical effect to a kinematical effect: *all physics must be conditioned such that it is invariant under Lorentz boosts*. In this way, the relativity principle could be reconciled with the Poincaré invariance of Maxwell's equations. Distinctive features of Einstein's approach include the following:

1. It eliminates 'asymmetries which do not appear to be inherent in the phenomena' (Einstein, 1905d). (Here, Einstein is referring to Lorentz's responses to the null ether wind results.)
2. It accounts for *all* null ether wind results.
3. It does not postulate an ether, or a standard of absolute rest, at all.
4. It is a 'principle theory' rather than a 'constructive theory'.

The idea is that when one boosts a material body with velocity v, one should (in light of the dynamics of that body – more on this below) take it that the boosted state is related to the original state by a Lorentz transformation rather than a Galilean transformation. In this way, one need not invoke dynamical contraction hypotheses in order to compensate for the fact that the velocity of light would differ in frames related by Galilean boosts. In other words, for Einstein, the theorists which preceded him had *misunderstood the nature of boosts*. Here is how Einstein put the matter:

> Examples of this sort, together with the unsuccessful attempts to discover any motion of the earth relatively to the 'light medium', suggest that the phenomena of electrodynamics as well as of mechanics possess no properties corresponding to the idea of absolute rest. They suggest rather that, as has already been shown to the first order of small quantities, the same laws of electrodynamics and optics will be valid for all frames of reference for which the equations of mechanics hold good. (Einstein, 1905d)

My purpose in this section is to dissect Einstein's 1905 derivation of the Lorentz transformations. Before doing so, however, I should say something on the aforementioned distinction between 'principle' and 'constructive' theories of physics.

4.1 Principle and Constructive Theories

The theory presented in Einstein's 1905 article is something which he would later recognise as a 'principle theory' rather than a 'constructive theory'. Einstein introduced this distinction in a 1919 article in the London *Times*:

> Most [theories in physics] are constructive. They attempt to build up a picture of the more complex phenomena out of the materials of a relatively simple formal scheme from which they start out. Thus, the kinetic theory of gases seeks to reduce mechanical, thermal, and diffusional processes to movements of molecules . . .
>
> [Principle theories, by contrast,] employ the analytic, not the synthetic method. The elements which form their basis and starting point are not hypothetically constructed but empirically discovered ones, general characteristics of natural processes, principles that give rise to mathematically formulated criteria which the separate processes . . . have to satisfy . . . The theory of relativity belongs to the latter class. (Einstein, 1919)

The distinction between principle and constructive theories Einstein presents in this passage can be cashed out thus:

Constructive theories: Theories which attempt to provide a detailed dynamical picture of what is microscopically going on, from which predictions for observable phenomena can be derived.
Principle theories: Theories which take certain phenomenologically well-grounded principles, raise them to the status of *postulates*, and derive from them constraints on what the underlying detailed dynamical equations could be like, without attempting to give a fully detailed account of what those equations *are*.

A paradigmatic example of a principle theory is thermodynamics; the 'phenomenologically well-grounded postulates' in this case are the laws of thermodynamics, from which one derives (say) relations between certain functions of state. The corresponding constructive theory in this case, as Einstein points out in this passage, would be the (statistical) kinetic theory of gases.

One might think constructive theories are superior to principle theories, in the sense that the former can provide deeper, mechanistic explanations for physical phenomena in a way the latter cannot. But in that case, why was Einstein's 1905 formulation of special relativity – which (in 1919) he declared a *principle* theory – so celebrated? One might be motivated to construct a principle theory by wanting to make *some* progress before the fully detailed microphysical picture (constructive account) is known. Einstein in 1905 saw himself as being in this situation: Lorentz had been pursuing a constructive approach, but Einstein was suspicious that the true equations governing intermolecular forces were a long way off.[22] It is, however, worth registering Einstein's reservations about principle theories:

> It seems to me . . . that a physical theory can be satisfactory only when it builds up its structures from elementary foundations. (Einstein, 1995)

> [W]hen we say we have succeeded in understanding a group of natural processes, we invariably mean that a constructive theory has been found which covers the processes in question. (Einstein, 1919)

4.2 Einstein's 1905 Article

Having recognised that Einstein was following the principle theory approach in his 1905 article – simply *assuming* (on the basis of phenomenological observations, e.g., no observed violations of the relativity principle) that the symmetry group for the laws of mechanics should be the same as the symmetry group for the laws of electromagnetism, without a clear understanding of the dynamics of matter which would underwrite this fact – I will now present Einstein's derivation of the Lorentz transformations as presented in his 1905 article.

Before I begin, there is one additional point to make. One might reasonably have questions about Einstein's methodology in his article. Since the Lorentz transformations were already known by 1905, what was Einstein adding to

---

[22] It does not have to be only historical circumstances which justify the use of principle theories – Einstein himself in his 1919 article points out that such theories have the merit of being connected directly with empirical experience and so of indubitability (here, there are interesting and under-explored connections with the programme of 'constructive axiomatics' promulgated by Reichenbach (1969): see Dewar, Linnemann, and Read (2022); Linnemann and Read (2021) for discussion). Moreover, certain explanatory factors may militate in favour of the use of principle theories – as Van Camp writes:

> Constructive theories are grounded in their ability to offer causal-mechanical explanations of phenomena, a type of scientific explanation most prominently advocated by Salmon (1984).
>   Principle theories are also explanatory. The primary function of a principle theory is tied to the explanatory role it plays through unification. The theory of explanation as unification was first advanced by Friedman (1974) and has been developed since by Kitcher (1989). (Van Camp, 2011, pp. 23–4)

For further discussion, see Read (2020b) and references therein.

extant knowledge? The point is that Lorentz *et al.* derived these transform-ations on the basis of detailed *dynamical* considerations. By contrast, Einstein would (a) proceed via phenomenological considerations regarding light and the relativity principle (and so would avoid having to make unjustified conjectures regarding underlying dynamics), and (b) would, as we have already seen, ele-vate the resulting transformations to a *kinematical constraint*. I will come back to these differences between Einstein and Lorentz.

4.2.1 Einstein's Operational Understanding of Coordinates

At the beginning of his article, Einstein is explicit that he has an *operational* understanding of coordinates. This understanding means he requires spatial coordinates to 'match' the length of rigid measuring rods that are at rest in the system in question, and time coordinates to 'match' the tickings of clocks at rest in that system. Einstein would come to regret this appeal to rigid rods and regular clocks in his articulation of his understanding of coordinates, as I will discuss in what follows (cf. Giovanelli, 2014); moreover and more gen-erally, Einstein would struggle throughout his career with how to understand coordinate systems (on this, see Giovanelli, 2021).

For my purposes in this subsection, I will follow Einstein in simply assuming this understanding of coordinates. Indeed and in any case, even to set up *one* coordinate system, we need more than this: we need to *decide* how to synchron-ise clocks that are spatially separated from one another. Having presented his understanding of coordinates, Einstein turns his attention to this very matter.

4.2.2 The Definition of Simultaneity

Consider the following set-up: two mirrors A and B are some fixed distance L apart. A photon is fired from A at event (i.e., spacetime point) A_1, bounces off B at B_2, and returns to A at A_3, as per Figure 4 (there, space runs along the horizontal axis and time along the vertical axis, as is standard). Now ask: which point on the worldline of mirror A is simultaneous with point B_2 on the worldline of mirror B? The natural answer stipulated by Einstein (following Poincaré) is the following (here 't_A' indicates the time read off by a clock at A; *mutatis mutandis* for B):

$$t_B(B_2) = t_A(A_1) + \frac{1}{2}(t_A(A_3) - t_A(A_1)). \tag{35}$$

That is, B_2 is simultaneous with the point *halfway* between A_1 and A_3 on A's worldline. This makes the one-way speed of light isotropic. (One would be perfectly within one's rights to ask whether this is the *only* way of 'spreading time through space' in special relativity—I will return to this issue in Section 8.)

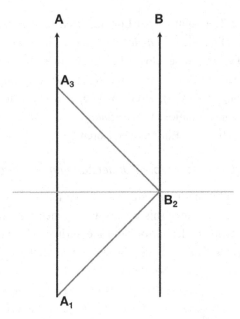

Figure 4 The 'light clock' set-up presented by Einstein (1905d)

For the time being, we can treat this as a *conventional choice* made by Einstein for how to synchronise distant clocks: typically, it is referred to as the *Einstein–Poincaré clock synchrony convention*.

4.2.3 Einstein's Two Postulates

We turn now to the main event: Einstein's two postulates of special relativity. These are the relativity principle (**RP**) (which we have already discussed at some length) and the light postulate (**LP**) (on which we also remarked in the previous section). As stated by Einstein, these read as follows:

RP: The laws by which the states of physical systems undergo change are not affected, whether these changes be referred to the one or the other of two systems of coordinates in uniform translatory motion.

LP: Any ray of light moves in the 'stationary' system of coordinates with the determined velocity c, whether the ray be emitted by a stationary or by a moving body. Hence

$$\text{velocity} = \frac{\text{light path}}{\text{time interval}},$$

where time interval is to be taken in the sense of the definition in Section 1.

Note that both **RP** and **LP** accord with the methodology of a principle theory: as we have already seen, (i) there were no empirically observed violations of **RP**, and (ii) light is a wave, so (like all waves) is such that the speed of the wave is independent of the speed of the source (which is **LP**). (Sometimes, **LP** is identified with the 'constancy of the speed of light', but this is not how the principle is stated. The constancy of the two-way speed of light *in inertial frames* follows from a combination of **RP** and **LP**; in non-inertial frames, the speed of light need not be c.) Einstein's point is going to be that (a) these conditions (plus the extra assumptions involved in the 1905 paper, namely those discussed elsewhere in this section) together imply that transformations between frames are the Lorentz transformations, and (b) if all material bodies are governed by equations which are invariant under these transformations, then one no longer predicts violations of **RP**, so there is no longer any need for a preferred frame, *a fortiori* no longer any need for an ether.

4.2.4 Homogeneity, Isotropy, and Reciprocity

The game is now to derive coordinate transformations from these principles, along with a couple of others. In particular, Einstein will also need to assume:

1. The homogeneity of space and time. ('Every point in space and time is the same as every other.')
2. The isotropy of space. ('There is no privileged direction in space.')

Note that homogeneity and isotropy are not equivalent: an example of an homogeneous but anisotropic space would be (say) a set of vectors all pointing in the same direction in a space; an example of an inhomogeneous but isotropic space would be one line γ, with vectors emanating radially from this line (in this case, the space is inhomogeneous, but isotropic about γ).

Also worthy of mention is the principle of 'Reciprocity', which states the following: if two inertial coordinate systems S and S' are such that S' is moving with speed v in the positive x direction relative to S, then S is moving with speed v in the negative x direction relative to S'. As Brown mentions, this principle holds if and only if the Einstein–Poincaré synchrony convention is adopted in both S and S' (Brown, 2005, p. 118). Von Ignatowski claimed Reciprocity follows from **RP** alone; however, in the absence of any stipulation regarding a clock synchrony convention, this claim is incorrect (Torretti, 1983, p. 79). Berzi and Gorini (1969), however, showed that Reciprocity *can* be derived from a combination of **RP** and spatial isotropy. Although these observations are independently interesting, the main point regarding Reciprocity I want to make is this: although the principle can be invoked at certain points in Einstein's derivation (see below), it is not necessary to take this as an independent assumption: rather, it can be derived from Einstein's other assumptions.

4.2.5 Linearity of the Transformations

Homogeneity implies that the transformations between inertial frames must be linear. Einstein does not spell this out, but a reconstruction can be found in Brown (2005, §2.3). Generic transformations between frames can be written

$$x'^{\mu} = f^{\mu}(x^{\nu}). \tag{36}$$

Suppose the transformations encode information on the behaviour of rods and clocks (recall Einstein's operational understanding of coordinate systems). Then such behaviour should not depend on where the rods and clocks find themselves in space or time, on pains of violation of homogeneity. Consider now the infinitesimal version of the transformation law,

$$dx'^{\mu} = \frac{\partial f^{\mu}}{\partial x^{\nu}} dx^{\nu}. \tag{37}$$

Homogeneity implies that the coefficients $\partial f^{\mu}/\partial x^{\nu}$ must be independent of the x^{ν} coordinates, which means f^{μ} must be linear functions of the coordinates x^{μ}.

4.2.6 Lorentz Transformations up to $\phi(v)$

Following Einstein, we now let K be a 'stationary' system and let (t, x, y, z) be coordinates for K, determined by the conditions of surveyability-using-rods-and-clocks-that-are-stationary-in-K and the Einstein definition of simultaneity applied in K (for t). We let k be a system of coordinates that is moving with speed v along the positive x-direction relative to the 'stationary' system K, and let (τ, ξ, η, ζ) be coordinates for k, determined by the conditions of surveyability-using-rods-and-clocks-that-are-stationary-in-k and the Einstein definition of simultaneity applied in k (for τ). Using Einsteinian synchrony in k and the linearity of the coordinate transformations, Einstein derives (I will omit his steps, since they are straightforward)

$$\tau = \phi(v)\gamma\left(t - \frac{vx}{c^2}\right). \tag{38}$$

Now consider a light ray emitted from the origin in the positive ξ-direction. Using **RP** and **LP** to write down expressions for the relationship between ξ and τ that holds on the path of this ray, and similarly (using **RP** alone) for the relationship between x and t that holds on the path of this ray, Einstein likewise derives that

$$\xi = \phi(v)\gamma(x - vt). \tag{39}$$

Similarly, by considering rays of light emitted in the η and ζ directions from the perspectives of both K and k, Einstein obtains

$$\eta = \phi(v)\,y, \tag{40}$$

$$\xi = \phi(v)\,z. \tag{41}$$

(38)–(41) are the Lorentz transformations up to a velocity-dependent factor $\phi(v)$.

4.2.7 Final Steps

The final steps involve setting $\phi(v) = 1$, and thereby recovering the Lorentz transformations. First, one invokes **RP** and Reciprocity in order to argue that $\phi(v)\,\phi(-v) = 1$. Now, given Einstein's operational understanding of coordinates, $\phi(v)$ can be interpreted physically as the inverse of the *transverse length contraction factor* – that is, the factor by which setting a body in motion causes that body to shrink in the direction perpendicular to its motion. Given that interpretation, isotropy entails that $\phi(v) = \phi(-v)$, so one has $\phi(v)^2 = 1$. We then argue somehow against the rogue possibility that $\phi(v) = -1$ (using continuity and $\phi(0) = +1?$ – Einstein does not discuss this explicitly). It then follows that $\phi(v) = 1$. This yields the by-now familiar Lorentz transformations!

4.3 Einstein versus the Trailblazers

Einstein's 1905 paper predicts once and for all the null result of ether wind experiments such as that of Michelson and Morley. Indeed, it does so *trivially* – just by insisting upon **RP** alongside **LP**. As I have already mentioned, one way to understand Einstein is as insisting that the laws of *mechanics* should also be Poincaré invariant – he is making Poincaré invariance universal, as a *kinematical constraint*. One sometimes finds the claim that Lorentz was not happy with Einstein's approach, as might seem apparent in passages such as the following:

> Einstein simply postulates what we have deduced, with some difficulty and not altogether satisfactorily, from the fundamental equations of the electromagnetic field. (Lorentz, 1892, p. 230)

To be fair to Lorentz, however, he followed this passage with this concession:

> By doing so, he may certainly take credit for making us see in the negative result of experiments like those of Michelson, Rayleigh and Brace, not a fortuitous compensation of opposing effects but the manifestation of a general and fundamental principle. (Lorentz, 1892, p. 230)

As Brown (2005, p. 68) writes, 'The full meaning of relativistic kinematics was simply not properly understood before Einstein'.

It is worth asking how radical Einstein's 1905 approach really was. Arguably, Newton himself was constructing a principle theory – the postulates being his three laws of motion. When combined with the **RP** and the auxiliary hypotheses mentioned in Section 2, these imply the Galilean invariance of physical laws (as a *kinematical constraint* – i.e., independent of the details of the particular dynamics governing matter). This indeed was achieved by Albert Keinstein in 1705: see Brown (2005, §3.3).[23]

> **Question:** Given the information provided in this section, was Einstein, in deriving a *different* kinematical constraint (*viz.*, Poincaré invariance, rather than Galilean invariance), really any more radical than Newton?

4.4 Einstein's Later Misgivings

Einstein would later voice certain misgivings about his 1905 derivation, in particular regarding:

1. The treatment of rods and clocks as primitive bodies, not 'moving atomic configurations'. (Einstein, 1921, 1969)
2. The special role of light. (Einstein, 1935, 1969)

On (1), here is what Einstein wrote in his *Autobiographical Notes*:

> One is struck [by the fact] that the theory [of special relativity] introduces two kinds of physical things, i.e. (1) measuring rods and clocks, (2) all other things, e.g., the electromagnetic field, the material point, etc. This, in a certain sense, is inconsistent; strictly speaking measuring rods and clocks would have to be represented as solutions of the basic equations (objects consisting of moving atomic configurations), not, as it were, as theoretically self-sufficient entities. However, the procedure justifies itself because it was clear from the very beginning that the postulates of the theory are not strong enough to deduce from them sufficiently complete equations . . . in order to base upon such a foundation a theory of measuring rods and clocks. . . . But one must not legalize the mentioned sin so far as to imagine that intervals are physical entities of a special type, intrinsically different from other variables ('reducing physics to geometry', etc.). (Einstein, 1969)

The point is that (as per its being a principle theory) Einstein's approach in 1905 simply assumes that boostable rods and clocks exist, which when boosted read of intervals as per a Lorentz transformed frame. Ultimately, this is a dynamical

---

[23] Please note that Keinstein is fictional!

assumption which should be justified rather than assumed: I will return to this issue in Section 7.

On (2), Einstein wrote this:

> The special theory of relativity grew out of the Maxwell electromagnetic equations. But... the Lorentz transformation, the real basis of special-relativity theory, in itself has nothing to do with the Maxwell theory. (Einstein, 1935)

> The Lorentz transformation transcended its connection with Maxwell's equations and had to do with the nature of space and time in general. (Brown, 2005, p. 73)

The point here is that the later Einstein viewed the appeal to Maxwell's electrodynamics in the 1905 paper as an heuristic tool into special relativity (based upon the historical contingency that the first Poincaré invariant laws discovered were Maxwell's), but in fact, once the completed theory of special relativity is in hand, one recognises that it has nothing *in particular* to do with electrodynamics. Here is how the later Einstein put the point:

> The content of the restricted relativity theory can accordingly be summarised in one sentence: all natural laws must be so conditioned that they are covariant with respect to Lorentz transformations. (Einstein, 1954)

4.5 The Ignatowski Transformations

In 1911, von Ignatowski sought to derive the Lorentz transformations using **RP**, but *without* **LP**. This claim should elicit suspicion: which of the remaining assumptions is violated by Newtonian physics (complete with Galilean transformations – cf. again the fable of Keinstein)? Let us delve into this. The Ignatowski transformations (i.e., those von Ignatowski derived in his 1911 article) read as follows, where K is some hitherto unspecified constant:

$$t' = \left(1 - Kv^2\right)^{-1/2} (t - Kvx),$$
$$\tag{42}$$

$$x' = \left(1 - Kv^2\right)^{-1/2} (x - vt),$$
$$\tag{43}$$

$$y' = y,$$
$$\tag{44}$$

$$z' = z.$$
$$\tag{45}$$

Note now three special cases:

- Setting $K = 0$ yields a Galilean transformation.
- Setting $K = 1$ yields a Lorentz transformation.
- Setting $K = -1$ yields a Euclidean transformation.

Recall that Galilean transformations consist of rigid three-dimensional spatial rotations, Galilean boosts, and rigid translations; Poincaré transformations consist of rigid three-dimensional spatial rotations, Lorentz boosts (together, these are the 'Lorentz transformations'), and rigid translations. We have not seen the four-dimensional Euclidean transformations up to this point, but these consist of rigid four-dimensional rotations plus rigid translations.

These results vindicate our suspicion: Galilean, Lorentz, and Euclidean transformations are thus *all* special cases of Ignatowski transformations. So dropping **LP** is not sufficient to derive the Lorentz transformations. Sometimes, authors rule out $K = -1$ as 'unphysical' (see, e.g., Pelissetto and Testa (2015)) – to this one should also object, for there are plenty of physical applications of theories with Euclidean symmetries – for example, any theory which uses the Poisson equation.[24]

5 Spacetime Structure

Up to this point, we have witnessed the crisis in physics which precipitated the advent of special relativity; we have also seen Einstein's derivation of the Lorentz transformations, the upshot of which was supposed to be that these transformations constitute a *kinematical constraint* on future physical theorising. So far, however, mention of spacetime has been conspicuously absent: we have not seen the term since Section 1!

It was only in 1909 that Minkowski showed that theories with Poincaré symmetries can be understood as being set in what has become known as *Minkowski spacetime*. In his paper, Minkowski introduced the 'world-postulate': the principle that all fundamental physical laws must be conditioned so as to be Poincaré invariant. This, as we have seen, was already to be found in Einstein, but by expressing this notion in four-dimensional geometrical language, Minkowski felt he had shown how 'the validity of the world-postulate ... now lies open in the full light of day' (Minkowski, 1909).

> **Question:** Can what Minkowski suggests here be understood as a precursor to a Friedman-style 'geometrical' approach to physical theories? (Cf. Section 1.)

My purpose in this section is to explain what this spatiotemporal structure amounts to, as well as to compare this structure with the Newtonian spacetime structures of which we already saw a little in Section 1. Before doing

---

[24] For further discussion on this point, see Read and Cheng (2022).

so, however, it is worth mentioning Einstein's initial reaction to Minkowski's spatiotemporal reformulation of special relativity. In response to Minkowski's somewhat grandiose claim that, having set theories in his spacetime, 'Henceforth space by itself, and time by itself, are doomed to fade away into mere shadows, and only a kind of union of the two will preserve an independent reality' (Minkowski, 1909), Einstein accused this work of being 'superfluous learnedness' (Pais, 1982). At the end of Section 6, I will consider what it even *means* for a theory to be 'special relativistic'; this reaction on the part of Einstein will be worth bearing in mind.

5.1 Two Conceptions of Geometry

Before introducing the specific details of Minkowski spacetime, we need to take a step back. In general, there are two different approaches to understanding geometrical notions: the 'Kleinian approach' and the 'Riemannian approach':[25]

Kleinian conception: Geometry is characterised via the invariance groups of certain structures under coordinate transformations.
Riemannian conception: Geometry is characterised via tensors and other coordinate-independent differential-geometric structures.

In this section, I will focus on the Kleinian approach and defer a discussion of the Riemannian approach to Section 6. The general idea of the Kleinian approach – from a physical point of view – is as follows. We have seen that the inertial frames are those coordinate systems in which dynamical equations governing matter take their simplest form and in which force-free particles move with uniform velocity. Sometimes, people also think about the inertial frames as those frames which respect spacetime's 'inertial structure' in a certain way. On the Kleinian approach, one can then use the transformations between the inertial frames of a theory to ascertain that theory's spacetime geometrical commitments. The three-point plan is this:

1. Specify the class of coordinate transformations which relate the inertial frames in the theory under consideration.
2. Identify the structures and quantities which are *invariant* under those transformations.
3. Regard these structures and quantities as picking out different kinds of spacetime.

---

[25] For more detail on the distinction between these two approaches, see Wallace (2019).

I am first going to illustrate how the Kleinian approach works in the case of Newtonian theories; after doing this, I will return to special relativity.

5.2 Spacetime Structure in Newtonian Physics

Perhaps surprisingly, the question of the spacetime structure of Newtonian mechanics turns out to be a delicate business – in fact, much *more* delicate than in the case of relativistic theories. There is indeed a hierarchy of possible 'classical' spacetime structures for Newtonian mechanics: running from strongest to weakest, this reads (Earman, 1989, ch. 2):

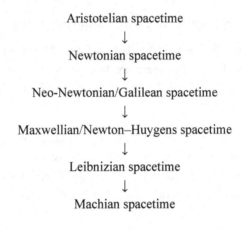

5.2.1 Aristotelian Spacetime

Let us begin with Aristotelian spacetime as conceived on the Kleinian approach.[26] Suppose one has a physical theory in which the dynamical equations take their simplest form in coordinate systems related by the following (rather restricted!) set of *Aristotelian transformations*:

$$t \mapsto \pm t + \tau \tag{46}$$

$$\mathbf{x} \mapsto \mathbf{R}\mathbf{x} \tag{47}$$

One now asks: what is preserved under such transformations? In this case, a great deal! The following structures are all invariants of these Aristotelian transformations:

1. A notion of spatial distance.
2. A notion of temporal distance.
3. A standard of rotation across time.
4. A notion of straightness of paths across time.

---

[26] Throughout the following, $\mathbf{R} \in SO\,(3)$ and any functions of t are smooth.

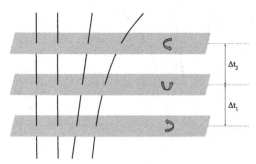

Figure 5 Aristotelian spacetime and the distinctions meaningful therein

5. A preferred velocity.
6. A preferred point.

In every case, the reason is that the structure in question is unaffected by time translations/inversions and/or spatial rotations – which exhaust the Aristotelian transformations. Given this, one can draw a picture of a spacetime which preserves all of these notions – see Figure 5. In this figure, let the vertical line on the left be the preferred point; anything co-moving with respect to the preferred point has the preferred velocity (and acceleration – i.e., standard of straightness of paths across time). In the spacetime, there is also a standard of rotation, allowing one to adjudicate on whether an object is spinning (this is represented by the curved arrows to the right); there is also a preferred notion of spatial distance at a time (on the grey hypersurfaces), and of temporal distance (between the grey hypersurfaces). Thus, respectively, absolute position, velocity, acceleration, rotation, temporal distance, and spatial distance are all well defined in Aristotelian spacetime.

5.2.2 Newtonian Spacetime

Suppose now that one liberalises the Aristotelian transformations to the following class of *Newtonian transformations*:

$$t \mapsto \pm t + \tau \tag{48}$$

$$\mathbf{x} \mapsto \mathbf{R}\mathbf{x} + \mathbf{a} \tag{49}$$

In particular, note that the Newtonian transformations – unlike the Aristotelian transformations – allow for constant translations of the spatial coordinates. This means a preferred point is no longer well defined in Newtonian spacetime, for such a point would not be left invariant by spatial translations! Thus, only the following concepts are well defined in Newtonian spacetime:

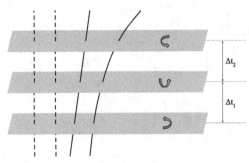

Figure 6 Newtonian spacetime, in which the universe has no preferred point

1. A notion of spatial distance.
2. A notion of temporal distance.
3. A standard of rotation across time.
4. A notion of straightness of paths across time.
5. A preferred velocity.
6. ~~A preferred point.~~

Accordingly, schematically, a picture of Newtonian spacetime might take the form presented in Figure 6. Here, the dashed lines are supposed to indicate that the two trajectories can be mapped into one another using the transformations of the Newton group, so there is no sense in this spacetime structure in which one is 'preferred' over the other. (In later diagrams in this section, the same rationale underlying the dashing applies.) Although here one no longer has a preferred point, one retains the trans-temporal identity of spacetime points *qua* spatial points, which affords a 'rigging' (i.e., congruence of vertical lines) with respect to which absolute velocity and acceleration can be defined.

5.2.3 Neo-Newtonian/Galilean Spacetime

Let us press on in the same spirit. Suppose one now liberalises the Newtonian transformations to the *Galilean transformations*:

$$t \mapsto \pm t + \tau \tag{50}$$

$$\mathbf{x} \mapsto \mathbf{R}\mathbf{x} + \mathbf{v}t + \mathbf{a} \tag{51}$$

Galilean transformations – unlike Newtonian transformations – now allow for constant velocity transformations of the spatial coordinates. This means a preferred velocity is no longer well defined in Galilean spacetime (sometimes called 'neo-Newtonian spacetime' – these terms are completely interchangeable), for such a velocity would not be preserved under Galilean

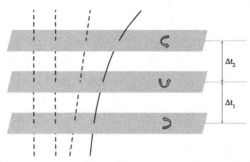

Figure 7 Galilean spacetime, in which there is no notion of absolute velocity

transformations! Thus, only the following concepts are well defined in Galilean spacetime:

1. A notion of spatial distance.
2. A notion of temporal distance.
3. A standard of rotation across time.
4. A notion of straightness of paths across time.
5. ~~A preferred velocity.~~
6. ~~A preferred point.~~

(Again, one can convince oneself that structures (1)–(4) are well defined in Galilean spacetime.) Schematically, a picture of Galilean spacetime would appear as in Figure 7. Here, the curved line is supposed to indicate that a standard of absolute acceleration remains in Galilean spacetime, even though one can map a vertical dashed line (i.e., the worldline of a body with some uniform velocity) to a non-vertical but straight dashed line (i.e., the worldline of a body with some other uniform velocity) by the action of the Galilean group. One might be puzzled by this: how can there be a standard of absolute acceleration, but not of absolute velocity? At this point, suffice it to say that this is a well-defined *mathematical* possibility; I hope to shed further light on this question in the following section, when I discuss the Riemannian approach to geometry.

5.2.4 Maxwellian/Newton–Huygens Spacetime

Next, suppose we liberalise the Galilean transformations to the *Maxwell transformations*:

$$t \mapsto \pm t + \tau \tag{52}$$

$$\mathbf{x} \mapsto \mathbf{R}\mathbf{x} + \mathbf{a}(t) \tag{53}$$

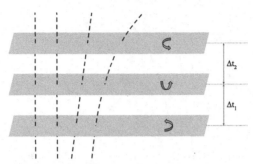

Figure 8 Maxwellian spacetime, in which there is no notion of absolute non-rotational acceleration

We now allow for arbitrary time-dependent transformations of the spatial coordinates. In this case, a preferred acceleration (i.e., standard of straightness of paths across time) is no longer well defined, for it is not preserved under such transformations. Thus, only the following concepts are well defined in Maxwellian/Newton–Huygens spacetime (again, the terms are completely interchangeable):

1. A notion of spatial distance.
2. A notion of temporal distance.
3. A standard of rotation across time.
4. ~~A notion of straightness of paths across time.~~
5. ~~A preferred velocity.~~
6. ~~A preferred point.~~

Schematically, a picture of Maxwellian spacetime might appear as in Figure 8. In this case, one can no longer distinguish between curved and straight lines through this spacetime structure.

5.2.5 Leibnizian Spacetime

Suppose we liberalise the Maxwell transformations to the *Leibniz transformations*:

$$t \mapsto \pm t + \tau \tag{54}$$

$$\mathbf{x} \mapsto \mathbf{R}(t)\mathbf{x} + \mathbf{a}(t) \tag{55}$$

In this case, we allow for arbitrary time-dependent *rotations* of the spatial coordinates. This means a standard of rotation is no longer well defined in Leibnizian spacetime, for rotation rate need not be left invariant under such transformations. Thus, only the following transformations are well defined in Leibnizian spacetime:

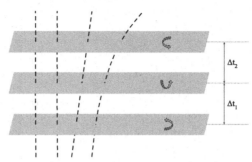

Figure 9 Leibnizian spacetime, in which there is no notion of absolute rotation

1. A notion of spatial distance.
2. A notion of temporal distance.
3. ~~A standard of rotation across time.~~
4. ~~A notion of straightness of paths across time.~~
5. ~~A preferred velocity.~~
6. ~~A preferred point.~~

Schematically, a picture of Leibnizian spacetime might then look appear as in Figure 9. Here, dashing of the curved arrows is supposed to indicate that there is no standard of rotation in Leibnizian spacetime.

5.2.6 Machian Spacetime

Now suppose we liberalise the Leibniz transformations to the *Machian transformations*:

$$t \mapsto f(t) \qquad (f \text{ monotonic}) \qquad (56)$$

$$\mathbf{x} \mapsto \mathbf{R}(t)\mathbf{x} + \mathbf{a}(t) \qquad (57)$$

We now allow for arbitrary rescalings of the temporal coordinates; this means a preferred notion of temporal distance is no longer well defined in Machian spacetime, for temporal distance is not an invariant of such transformations. Thus, only the following transformations are well defined in Machian spacetime:

1. A notion of spatial distance.
2. ~~A notion of temporal distance.~~
3. ~~A standard of rotation across time.~~
4. ~~A notion of straightness of paths across time.~~
5. ~~A preferred velocity.~~
6. ~~A preferred point.~~

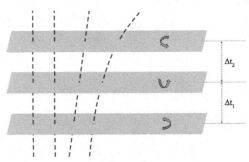

Figure 10 Machian spacetime, in which there is no notion of absolute temporal duration

Schematically, a picture of Machian spacetime might appear as in Figure 10. Here, dashing of the temporal intervals between spatial hypersurfaces is supposed to indicate that such intervals are not invariants of the Machian transformations.

5.2.7 Summary

This constitutes the standard hierarchy of classical spacetimes, as one finds in, for example, Earman (1989, ch. 2). I think it suffices by now to illustrate the general point: as one liberalises one's class of allowed transformations (which, physically, are to be understood as relating the frames of reference in which one's description of the physics takes its simplest form), the number of invariants of those transformations decreases; thus, one's spacetime geometrical structure (understood as per the Kleinian approach) becomes, in a clear sense, weaker. The general moral here is worth keeping in mind:

> More symmetries $\Longleftrightarrow$ Less structure

Also worthy of mention is that there are other possible elements of the hierarchy of classical spacetimes which I have elided on the grounds that they are not necessary to make these points. First: one might allow reflections of the spatial coordinates, so $x \mapsto \pm x$; in this case, spacetime would no longer have a preferred spatial *orientation* (see, e.g., Huggett (2000)). Second: one might allow for *rescalings* of the spatial coordinates: $x \mapsto \Omega x$ (here, Ω is a matrix implementing a possibly spacetime-dependent scale transformation); in this case, only spatial *conformal structure* (i.e., angles, but not distances) would be well defined.[27]

---

[27] The resulting spacetime has a claim to be the correct spacetime structure for the programme of 'shape dynamics' (Read, 2023). For more on shape dynamics, see Mercati (2018).

5.3 Spacetime Structure in Special Relativity

By now, I have spent a lot of time presenting different classical spacetime structures through the lens of the Kleinian approach. At this point, we must ask: how does the spacetime structure of special relativity compare with that of the spacetimes we have just seen? To answer this question, it is helpful to switch notation. Consider again the coordinate transformations associated with Galilean spacetime. So far, I have written these in vector notation, as in (50) and (51). The equivalent expressions in *index notation* would be

$$t \mapsto \pm t + \tau \tag{58}$$

$$x^i \mapsto R^i{}_j x^j + v^i t + a^i \tag{59}$$

Note that all terms must have the same free indices, and the Einstein summation convention is used (so that indices which appear twice in a term are summed over). By convention, we use Latin indices ($i, j, \ldots = 1, 2, 3$) for spatial indices, and Greek indices ($\mu, \nu, \ldots = 0, 1, 2, 3$) for space*time* indices.

With this in mind, we can present the *Poincaré transformations* as follows:

$$x^\mu \mapsto \Lambda^\mu{}_\nu x^\nu + a^\mu \qquad (\Lambda^\mu{}_\nu \in SO(1,3)). \tag{60}$$

The spacetime structure left invariant under the action of the Poincaré transformations *just is* the spacetime structure Minkowski introduced in 1909. In this *Minkowski spacetime*, there is:

1. ~~A notion of spatial distance.~~
2. ~~A notion of temporal distance.~~
3. A standard of rotation across time.
4. A notion of straightness of paths across time.
5. ~~A preferred velocity.~~
6. ~~A preferred point.~~
7. A notion of *spacetime* distance.

Note that what is well defined and what is not in Minkowski spacetime cuts across the classical hierarchy: in all of our classical spacetimes, there was a well-defined notion of spatial distance; by contrast, this is *not* an invariant of the Poincaré transformations. By contrast, there *is* a preferred notion of straightness of paths across time (translating into a notion of absolute acceleration), *unlike* (e.g.) Maxwellian, Leibnizian, or Machian spacetime. On the other hand, one very important invariant of the Poincaré transformations is the *interval* – a notion of four-dimensional spacetime distance, which can be written

$$I = -c^2 dt^2 + dx^2 + dy^2 + dz^2. \tag{61}$$

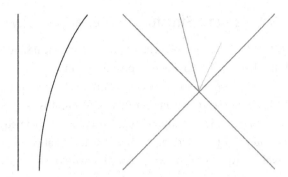

Figure 11 The (schematic) structure of Minkowksi spacetime

The interval I is preserved in all inertial frames in special relativity – that is, in all frames related by Poincaré transformations. It can be used to distinguish between three different kinds of trajectory through spacetime:

1. *Timelike* paths (representing the trajectories of massive bodies), which are such that the tangent vector to the path at every point is such that $I < 0$.
2. *Spacelike* paths (representing the trajectories of superluminal bodies), which are such that the tangent vector to the path at every point is such that $I > 0$.
3. *Null* paths (representing the trajectories of massless bodies such as light rays), which are such that the tangent vector to the path at every point is such that $I = 0$.

Together, these three kinds of trajectory pick out the famous 'lightcone' structure of special relativity. Schematically, then, a picture of Minkowski spacetime might appear as in Figure 11. What I mean by this figure is the following. The two lines on the left indicate that one can still distinguish straight (i.e., non-accelerating) from curved (i.e., accelerating) paths through this spacetime (one also has a standard of rotation in Minkowski spacetime, but I have not represented that in the diagram). On the right, the cross represents the lightcone structure of the theory; the two lines within the forward 'lobe' of the cross represent two distinct timelike vectors.

5.4 Further Reflections on Spacetime

Up to this point, I have introduced both the hierarchy of classical spacetimes, as well as Minkowski spacetime, via the Kleinian approach. I will close this section with some further philosophical points regarding the nature of spacetime. The first regards the connection between spacetime and dynamical laws.

In Section 2, we saw that the laws of Newtonian mechanics are invariant under Galilean transformations. But these are the transformations associated with Galilean spacetime, as we have seen. It is natural, therefore, to regard Newtonian mechanics as *set in Galilean spacetime*. Earman (1989, ch. 3) makes it a very general principle that the spacetime and dynamical symmetries of a theory should match, by laying down the following two conditions:[28]

SP1: Any dynamical symmetry of T is a spacetime symmetry of T.
SP2: Any spacetime symmetry of T is a dynamical symmetry of T.

The idea is this: if there are dynamical symmetries which are not spacetime symmetries, then (by our mantra that 'more symmetries' is equivalent to 'less structure') there is spatiotemporal structure which is not relevant to the dynamics. In that case, by an Occamist norm, such structure should be expunged. On the other hand, if there are spacetime symmetries which are not dynamical symmetries, then it seems that one's dynamics adverts to structures which do not exist. It is questionable whether this is even coherent: Belot (2000) calls it 'arrant knavery'.[29]

In this sense, one might accuse Newton of having made a mistake in postulating that Newtonian rather than Galilean spacetime is the correct spacetime setting for his theory. The thought here is that we have neither *a priori* nor *direct* empirical access to the structure of spacetime we live in; rather, our guide to which structure obtains is in the dynamical laws: we should postulate as much structure as is required to state (the invariance properties of) the laws of our best physical theories, *and no more*. (To repeat, this is essentially the content of Earman's conditions.) With hindsight, Newton violated this requirement: Newtonian physics can be formulated in (merely) *Galilean* spacetime, not *Newtonian* spacetime (as Newton maintained). Occam's razor thus advises against postulating a standard of absolute rest in addition.[30]

Raising this point presents the following question: is it indeed the case that *Galilean* spacetime is the correct spacetime setting for Newtonian mechanics (given Earman's conditions), as is by now the standard line? If we follow the methodology of moving from Newtonian to Galilean spacetime as the correct spacetime setting for Newtonian mechanics, then (it seems) the discovery of *further* symmetries of the Newtonian laws would likewise motivate moving

---

[28] Myrvold (2019) has gone further, arguing these principles are *analytically true* (cf. Acuña 2016). I will return to this suggestion in Section 7.

[29] For what it is worth, I disagree with Belot's claims that such approaches are incoherent. For example, Huggett's regularity relationalism (2006) – recall Section 1 – begins with an impoverished spacetime ontology yet gives a precise prescription for how further spatiotemporal commitments may be secured via dynamical considerations.

[30] While this might be true in principle, I agree with Dasgupta (2016) that in practice, since Newton did not have the concept of Galilean spacetime, he was justified in believing in Newtonian absolute space and thereby in violating Earman's principles.

to a different spacetime setting again, with even less structure than Galilean spacetime. With this in mind, consider Newton's 'Corollary VI' in the *Principia*:

> If bodies moved in any manner among themselves are urged, in the direction of parallel lines by equal accelerative forces, they will all continue to move among themselves, after the same manner as if they had not been urged by those forces. (Cajori, 1934, p. 21)

This points out that there is no standard of *linear* acceleration in Newtonian mechanics – so perhaps the correct spacetime setting for the theory should be *Maxwellian* spacetime. This suggestion was raised by Saunders (2013) and remains controversial – see, for example, Knox (2014) and Wallace (2020).

The second point I wish to make is this. If we impose extra structure on Galilean spacetime (namely, a standard of rest), we can recover Newtonian spacetime. Perhaps more surprisingly, however, if we impose extra structure on Minkowski spacetime (namely, again, a standard of rest), we can *also* recover Newtonian spacetime. So, as Barrett summarises:

> There is a precise sense in which Newtonian spacetime has more structure than both Galilean spacetime and Minkowski spacetime. But in this same sense, Galilean and Minkowski spacetime have incomparable amounts of structure; neither spacetime has less structure than the other. The progression towards a less structured spacetime therefore does not continue into the relativistic setting. (Barrett, 2015, p. 37)

6 General Covariance

In this section, I am going to explain how the second of our two approaches to geometry – the Riemannian approach – works. Ultimately, I will return to both the classical hierarchy and Minkowski spacetime. Before doing so, however, I need to say a little more on the different ways in which one might present a given set of physical laws.

6.1 Physical Laws

In the previous section, I introduced briefly the four-dimensional index notation. Let us now consider how to write some familiar physical laws using this index notation. I will begin with the free, massless Klein–Gordon equation, which is a four-dimensional wave equation for a scalar field ϕ:

$$-\frac{1}{c^2}\frac{\partial^2\phi}{\partial t^2} + \frac{\partial^2\phi}{\partial x^2} + \frac{\partial^2\phi}{\partial y^2} + \frac{\partial^2\phi}{\partial z^2} = 0. \tag{62}$$

Completely equivalently, I can write this equation using a matrix, as follows:

$$\left(\begin{matrix} \frac{1}{c}\frac{\partial}{\partial t} & \frac{\partial}{\partial x} & \frac{\partial}{\partial y} & \frac{\partial}{\partial z} \end{matrix} \right) \begin{pmatrix} -1 & & & \\ & 1 & & \\ & & 1 & \\ & & & 1 \end{pmatrix} \begin{pmatrix} \frac{1}{c}\frac{\partial}{\partial t} \\ \frac{\partial}{\partial x} \\ \frac{\partial}{\partial y} \\ \frac{\partial}{\partial z} \end{pmatrix} \phi = 0. \tag{63}$$

Calling the vector of partial derivatives ∂^μ ($\mu = 0 \ldots 3$) and the matrix $\eta_{\mu\nu}$, I can again write this (completely equivalently!) using the Einstein summation convention (where, recall again, repeated indices are summed) as follows:

$$\eta_{\mu\nu}\partial^\mu\partial^\nu\phi = 0. \tag{64}$$

It is important to stress that the content of (64) is *exactly the same* as that of (62): it still describes the same behaviour of the field ϕ, in the same coordinate system. Yet there are merits to the latter syntactic formulation: not only does it save ink, but (as we will see shortly), it also helps us to ascertain the symmetries of this equation (a point to which I alluded in Section 2).

Before I get onto this, I will introduce a couple more examples. Consider the Newton–Poisson equation, which describes the gravitational potential ϕ in the field formulation of Newtonian gravity (here ρ is the mass density field):

$$\frac{\partial^2\phi}{\partial x^2} + \frac{\partial^2\phi}{\partial y^2} + \frac{\partial^2\phi}{\partial z^2} = 4\pi\rho. \tag{65}$$

As before, I can rewrite this equation using a matrix as follows:

$$\left(\begin{matrix} \frac{1}{c}\frac{\partial}{\partial t} & \frac{\partial}{\partial x} & \frac{\partial}{\partial y} & \frac{\partial}{\partial z} \end{matrix} \right) \begin{pmatrix} 0 & & & \\ & 1 & & \\ & & 1 & \\ & & & 1 \end{pmatrix} \begin{pmatrix} \frac{1}{c}\frac{\partial}{\partial t} \\ \frac{\partial}{\partial x} \\ \frac{\partial}{\partial y} \\ \frac{\partial}{\partial z} \end{pmatrix} \phi = 4\pi\rho. \tag{66}$$

Defining ∂^μ exactly as before, and now calling the matrix $h^{\mu\nu}$, I can write this equation as follows, where the Einstein summation convention is used:

$$h^{\mu\nu}\partial_\mu\partial_\nu\phi = 4\pi\rho. \tag{67}$$

Again, it bears stressing that the content of (67) is *exactly the same* as the content of (65). Moreover, the advantages of this formulation are the same as in the previous case: (i) it is more compact, and (ii) it is easier to use this formulation to ascertain the symmetries of the equation than the first.

The third example is particularly relevant to special relativity: Maxwell's equations. Recall again that, in the usual three-vector presentation, these equations read:

$$\nabla \cdot \mathbf{E} = \rho, \tag{68}$$

$$\nabla \cdot \mathbf{B} = 0, \tag{69}$$

$$\nabla \times \mathbf{E} = -\frac{\partial \mathbf{B}}{\partial t}, \tag{70}$$

$$\nabla \times \mathbf{B} = \mathbf{J} + \frac{\partial \mathbf{E}}{\partial t}. \tag{71}$$

If I define the following two objects:

$$F^{\mu\nu} = \begin{pmatrix} 0 & -E_1/c & -E_2/c & -E_3/c \\ E_1/c & 0 & -B_3 & B_2 \\ E_2/c & B_3 & 0 & -B_1 \\ E_3/c & -B_2 & B_1 & 0 \end{pmatrix}, \tag{72}$$

$$J^{\mu} = \begin{pmatrix} \rho \\ J^i \end{pmatrix}, \tag{73}$$

then Maxwell's equations can be written:

$$\eta_{\mu\lambda}\partial^{\lambda}F^{\mu\nu} = J^{\nu}, \tag{74}$$

$$\partial_{\mu}F_{\nu\lambda} + \partial_{\nu}F_{\lambda\mu} + \partial_{\lambda}F_{\mu\nu} =: \partial_{[\mu}F_{\nu\lambda]} = 0. \tag{75}$$

As before, at this stage, (74) and (75) are simply a compact and convenient reformulation of our initial version of equations (68)–(71).

Exercise: Plug components into (74) and (75) in order to recover Maxwell's equations in their three-vector forms, (68)–(71).

Having put all these examples on the table, let us think about the second professed advantage: that the latter (more compact) formulations make it easier to ascertain the symmetries of these equations. The Klein–Gordon and Maxwell theories both feature explicit coupling to $\eta_{\mu\nu}$. The simplest form of these equations will be preserved under coordinate transformations which preserve the diagonal form of $\eta_{\mu\nu}$ – that is, coordinate transformations such that $\Lambda^{\sigma}{}_{\mu}\Lambda^{\lambda}{}_{\nu}\eta_{\sigma\lambda} = \eta_{\mu\nu}$. But these are just the Lorentz transformations!

Exercise: Verify that the condition $\Lambda^{\sigma}{}_{\mu}\Lambda^{\lambda}{}_{\nu}\eta_{\sigma\lambda} = \eta_{\mu\nu}$ picks out Lorentz boosts and/or spatial rotations.

Indeed, the equations are also invariant under translations, making them invariant under the full Poincaré group. One sometimes hears the claim that writing a theory using four-dimensional indices makes the symmetries of one's equations 'manifest' – this can be misleading, but the point is that it is easier to read off the symmetries of equations when they are formulated in this way.

> **Exercise:** Show explicitly that the Klein–Gordon equation (64) and Maxwell equations (74)–(75) are invariant under Poincaré transformations.

We can use exactly the same methodology to demonstrate the Galilean invariance of the Newton–Poisson equation (67). This equation features explicit coupling to $h^{\mu\nu}$. The simplest form of this equation will be preserved under coordinate transformations which preserve the diagonal form of $h^{\mu\nu}$ – that is, coordinate transformations such that $M^{\mu}{}_{\sigma} M^{\nu}{}_{\lambda} h^{\sigma\lambda} = h^{\mu\nu}$. Assuming that the transformations are linear (i.e., assuming that the change-of-basis matrices $M^{\mu}{}_{\sigma}$ are not functions of spacetime coordinates), these are just the Galilean transformations (up to a constant rescaling of t^{31}), once we also include translations.[32]

> **Exercise:** Show explicitly that the Newton–Poisson equation (67) is invariant under Galilean transformations.

The point to stress here is that so far we have just *repackaged* these dynamical equations – we have not fundamentally changed their symmetry properties. In fact, the index notation makes it pretty easy to transform to an arbitrary coordinate system and see these equations in their general (and ugly!) form: indeed I did this explicitly in the case of **N1L** in Section 1.

> **Exercise:** Transform (1) to arbitrary coordinates and thereby reproduce (3) from Section 1.

One can also show this in the case of, for example, the Klein–Gordon equation: explicitly, the transformation proceeds as follows:

$$\eta_{\mu\nu}\partial^{\mu}\partial^{\nu}\varphi = 0$$

$$\eta_{\mu\nu}\frac{\partial}{\partial x_{\mu}}\frac{\partial}{\partial x_{\nu}}\varphi = 0$$

---

[31] If one considers the symmetries of the Newton–Poisson equation only, one in fact finds that the allowed transformations of the temporal coordinate are $t \mapsto \kappa t$ for some constant κ; one can only set $\kappa = \pm 1$ if one assumes that the symmetries in addition preserve a standard of temporal distance, which, strictly speaking, is not part of the content of the Newton–Poisson equation.

[32] If one liberalises the linearity condition, one finds that (67) is in fact invariant under the Leibniz group of transformations. This is not so surprising once one notes that (67) is a static, three-dimensional equation, so changes in the temporal direction should leave it unchanged. When one also considers the force equation of Newtonian gravity, the symmetry group of the theory is restricted.

$$\longrightarrow \eta_{\mu\nu}\frac{\partial x_{\mu'}}{\partial x_\mu}\frac{\partial}{\partial x_{\mu'}}\left(\frac{\partial x_{\nu'}}{\partial x_\nu}\frac{\partial}{\partial x_{\nu'}}\varphi\right)=0$$

$$\eta_{\mu\nu}\frac{\partial x_{\mu'}}{\partial x_\mu}\left(\frac{\partial^2 x_{\nu'}}{\partial x_{\mu'}\partial x_\nu}\frac{\partial}{\partial x_{\nu'}}\varphi+\frac{\partial x_{\nu'}}{\partial x_\nu}\frac{\partial}{\partial x_{\mu'}}\frac{\partial}{\partial x_{\nu'}}\varphi\right)=0$$

$$\eta_{\mu\nu}\frac{\partial^2 x_{\nu'}}{\partial x_\mu\partial x_\nu}\partial^{\nu'}\varphi+\eta_{\mu\nu}\frac{\partial x_{\mu'}}{\partial x_\mu}\frac{\partial x_{\nu'}}{\partial x_\nu}\partial^{\mu'}\partial^{\nu'}\varphi=0.$$

Note the extra term in the non-inertial frame (cf. fictitious forces in (3)).

6.2 General Covariance

Can we write theories in what is known as a *generally covariant* form – that is, a form which holds in an arbitrary frame? (Note that the terminology 'general *c*ovariance' is confusing here – it should really be 'general *in*variance', but to mesh with the literature I will use the standard term.) Einstein circa 1915 thought the answer to this question was *no*, and that this is what made his newly developed general relativity special. But Kretschmann said in 1917 to Einstein: *yes*. Indeed, speaking anachronistically, there are (at least) two different ways to render a theory generally covariant:[33]

1. Write its equations in an arbitrary frame, with all extra terms included.
2. Write the theory in a *coordinate-independent* language.

We have seen (1) both with moving from equation (1) to equation (3) and with our transformation of the Klein–Gordon equation to an arbitrary frame. Let us now think a bit more about (2). To do this, we need to be clear about the distinction between (i) geometric objects and (ii) the components of those objects in a given coordinate system.

To illustrate this difference, consider a vector which I will call v^a: the components of this vector in one given (Cartesian) coordinate system could be as per Figure 12. If I now rotate the coordinate system (i.e., do a passive transformation), the vector will remain unchanged, but its components will differ, perhaps as per Figure 13.

One might, in light of this, seek to write down *different* dynamical equations for a physical theory, which are liberated altogether from coordinate systems, and which treat with geometric objects themselves, rather than the representations of those objects in some coordinate system.[34] To write a theory in a coordinate-independent way, we move from using *coordinate indices* ($\mu, \nu, \ldots$), which represent the *components* of objects in a particular coordinate

---

[33] For historical background, see Norton (1993).
[34] For some reflections on whether this is always possible, see Pitts (2012); Read (2022).

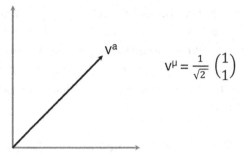

Figure 12 A vector v^a and its components v^μ in some coordinate system

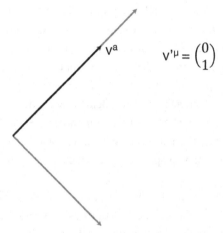

Figure 13 A vector v^a and its components v'^μ in a distinct coordinate system

basis, to *abstract indices* $(a, b, \ldots)$, which directly represent the objects them-selves. For example, in the case of the Klein–Gordon equation, move from (64) to

$$\eta_{ab} \nabla^a \nabla^b \phi = 0. \tag{76}$$

This involves no reference to a coordinate system at all – so it *a fortiori* holds in all coordinate systems. Note in particular that in order to make this move, we have introduced two *new* objects: (what is known as) a rank-2 tensor field η_{ab}, and a derivative operator ∇. Suffice it to say that both of these objects can be defined in a coordinate-independent manner (Friedman, 1983; Malament, 2012).

This move is not always metaphysically innocent. Sometimes, one finds the claim that writing our theories in a coordinate-independent language makes manifest the full ontological commitments of those theories. For example, in the case of Klein–Gordon theory, the claim would be that coordinate-independent presentations make manifest the commitment of the theory not merely to the field ϕ, but also to another field, η_{ab} – Minkowski space-time (along with its compatible derivative operator ∇ – 'compatible' means $\nabla_a \eta_{bc} = 0$). But should this be regarded as representing an autonomous entity (i.e., object in our ontology), or just as being a *codification* of the symmetries of the coordinate-based dynamical equations from which we began? I will return to this issue in detail in Section 7.

6.3 The Riemannian Conception of Geometry

Rather than identifying geometrical structures as the invariants of a given set of transformations (as per the Kleinian approach), the Riemannian approach directly presents and defines such structures without any reference to coordinate systems (the technical details of how this works are often sophisticated, but see, e.g., Friedman, 1983 and Malament, 2012 for explicit presentations of how objects of the kind I will discuss in the remainder of this section can be defined on the Riemannian approach).[35] The Kleinian and Riemannian approaches are complementary, insofar as the transformations specified in the Kleinian approach are those transformations which would leave invariant the structures presented on the Riemannian approach, were they to be written in a coordinate basis.

For the time being, I will simply present the Riemannian approach, first to the hierarchy of classical spacetime structures we saw in Section 5, and then to special relativity. To begin, recall again that the following structures are well defined in Aristotelian spacetime:

1. A notion of spatial distance.
2. A notion of temporal distance.
3. A standard of rotation across time.
4. A notion of straightness of paths across time.
5. A preferred velocity.
6. A preferred point.

To underwrite these notions, on the Riemannian approach, we specify Aristotelian spacetime as a tuple of geometric objects, $\langle M, t_{ab}, h^{ab}, \nabla, \sigma^a, \xi \rangle$. Here, M is a four-dimensional differentiable manifold representing the points of spacetime; t_{ab} is a temporal metric field of signature $(1, 0, 0, 0)$ which represents temporal distance relations between spacetime points; h^{ab} is a spatial metric field of signature $(0, 1, 1, 1)$ representing spatial distance relations between

---

[35] Whether the Riemannian approach *really* makes no appeal to coordinate systems is questionable – see Wallace (2019)—but I will set this aside here.

spacetime points; ∇ is a derivative operator affording standards both of straightness of paths and of rotations; σ^a is a timelike (in the sense that $t_{ab}\sigma^b \neq 0$) vector field representing trans-temporal identities of spacetime points *qua* spatial points and affording a standard of rest; and ξ is a scalar field identifying the preferred point in this spacetime. (As I say, I will not go further into the technical details here, but interested readers should consult, e.g., Earman, 1989; Friedman, 1983; Malament, 2012.)

As one weakens the spacetime structure in the classical hierarchy, fewer and fewer geometrical notions become meaningful, as we have already seen. This is captured easily in the Riemannian approach: one simply defines fewer and fewer geometrical objects in one's spacetime models. Using the same objects as before, the entire classical hierarchy can be captured as follows:

Aristotelian spacetime: $\langle M, t_{ab}, h^{ab}, \nabla, \sigma^a, \xi \rangle$
Newtonian spacetime: $\langle M, t_{ab}, h^{ab}, \nabla, \sigma^a \rangle$
Galilean spacetime: $\langle M, t_{ab}, h^{ab}, \nabla \rangle$
Maxwellian spacetime: $\langle M, t_{ab}, h^{ab}, [\nabla] \rangle$
Leibnizian spacetime: $\langle M, t_{ab}, h^{ab} \rangle$
Machian spacetime: $\langle M, h^{ab} \rangle$

There are a couple of further points to make at this stage. First: as already mentioned, it is now Galilean spacetime which (for better or worse) is regarded as the 'correct' spacetime setting for Newtonian mechanics. It is for this reason that authors such as Malament (2012) simply present Newtonian gravity in this setting, without identifying Galilean spacetime by name. Second: one might wonder what the square brackets are doing in the presentation of Maxwellian spacetime. Typically, when one sees such notation in mathematics, what is meant is an *equivalence class* of the relevant object (within the brackets). In this case, $[\nabla]$ denotes the equivalence class of derivative operators ∇ which differ on their standards of linear acceleration (i.e., differ on the adjudications of which one-dimensional paths through spacetime are bent – i.e., accelerating), but which agree on their standard of rotation (i.e., agree in the adjudications of whether bodies are rotating). Thus, by taking this equivalence class, we secure exactly the structure we defined in the previous section to be implicated in Maxwellian spacetime – and no more.

As another example in which the same notation appears, typically conformal structure – which encodes facts about angles but not facts about distances – is written in the Riemannian approach using square brackets. For example, one might yet further weaken Machian spacetime to encode only conformal structure on the spacelike hypersurfaces: in this case, one could write the models of the theory as $\langle M, [h^{ab}]\rangle$. Now, in all such cases, one might complain that it would be better (in the sense of: more physically perspicuous) to define geometric objects such that exactly as much structure as required is introduced from the outset, rather than by (a) introducing something with too much structure, then (b) telling us to forget about some of it. I agree![36] Indeed, Weatherall (2018) has shown recently that it is possible to write Maxwellian spacetime using a 'standard of rotation' $\circlearrowleft$ which meets this desideratum. Thus, in fact, it would arguably be better – and more physically/metaphysically perspicuous – to write the models of Maxwellian spacetime as $\langle M, t_{ab}, h^{ab}, \circlearrowleft \rangle$.[37]

6.4 What Is Special Relativity?

By now, we understand (i) the genesis of special relatvity, (ii) the content of Einstein's 1905 paper, and (iii) the different senses in which one might understand the spatiotemporal commitments of physical theories, including special relativity. But, having achieved all this, the following question arises naturally: just *what is* special relativity? In fact, there are at least three different options on the table:

1. Special relativity consists of the **RP**, the **LP**, whatever supplementary principles are needed to derive the Lorentz transformations therefrom, and said derivation of the Lorentz transformations.
2. Special relativity is the statement that the laws of physics (in standard formulation) are Poincaré invariant.
3. Special relativity is the statement that spacetime structure (over and above topological and differentiable structure) is exhausted by Minkowski spacetime.

In the coming sections of this Element, we will see how different views on the nature of special relativity can have substantial impacts upon one's preferred resolution to certain philosophical puzzles which arise in that theory (however construed).

> **Question:** Which of these options do you think best captures the 'essence' of special relativity? Or is this a wrong-headed question, and, if so, why?

---

[36] Here, there are connections to a recent philosophical debate about 'sophistication': see Dewar (2019); Martens and Read (2020).

[37] In the case of conformal structure, one can use a tensor density – see, for example, Linnemann and Read (2021).

7 Dynamical and Geometrical Approaches

One of the central and recurring themes of this Element regards the profound differences between 'dynamical' and 'geometrical' approaches, both to articulating the content of physical theories (e.g., Newtonian mechanics – see Section 1) and to the explanations of physical phenomena (e.g., the twin paradox time differential – see Section 10). In this section, I will address head-on some of the central differences between authors in these two camps (while also recognising that there are substantial differences *internal* to each of these camps).[38]

7.1 Bell's Lorentzian Pedagogy

John Bell, in his famous article 'How to Teach Special Relativity' (2004), considers an atom as modelled by classical Maxwell theory. He shows that, when such an atom is accelerated gently up to some constant velocity, its moving state will be contracted with respect to its stationary state, in accordance with the length contraction of subsystems under active Lorentz boosts. The moral – what he calls *Lorentzian pedagogy* – is that we can *explain* the behaviour of macroscopic systems via appeal to the micro-dynamical underpinnings of those systems. In particular, we can do so without 'premature philosophizing about space and time' (Bell, 2004).

Brown and Pooley (2001) take inspiration from Bell's Lorentzian pedagogy: they maintain that appeal to the fundamental physical laws governing the systems under consideration can explain the behaviour of those systems. I will come back to this in a minute, but for the time being note that Bell himself stresses that there are some limitations to his particular electron model as a means of illustrating the Lorentzian pedagogy:

> Can we conclude then that an arbitrary system, set in motion, will show precisely the Fitzgerald and Larmor effects? Not quite. There are two provisos to be made.
>
> The first is this: the Maxwell–Lorentz theory provides a very inadequate model of actual matter, in particular solid matter. It is not possible in a classical model to reproduce the empirical stability of such matter. . . .
>
> The second proviso is this. Lorentz invariance alone shows that for any state of a system at rest there is a corresponding 'primed' state of that system in motion. But it does not tell us that if the system is set anyhow in motion, it will actually go into the 'prime' of the original state, rather than into the 'prime' of some other state of the system at rest. In fact, it will generally

---

[38] For more on this debate, see Brown and Read (2021); Huggett, Hoefer, and Read (2022); Read (2020a, 2020b).

do the latter. A system set brutally in motion may be bruised, or broken, or heated, or burned. (Bell, 2004, pp. 74–5)

Here, Bell is stressing that, in order for the Lorentzian pedagogy to go through in full detail, we had better

1. appeal to the fundamental laws governing the physical systems under consideration, and
2. hope we can actually build stable bodies (such as rods and clocks) from matter governed by such laws.[39]

In a sense, this point is not novel to Bell. Here is Pauli, writing on the selfsame issues:

> Should one, then, completely abandon any attempt to explain the Lorentz contraction atomistically? We think that the answer to this question should be No. The contraction of a measuring rod is not an elementary but a very complicated process. It would not take place except for the covariance with respect to the Lorentz group of the basic equations of electron theory, as well as of those laws, as yet unknown to us, which determine the cohesion of the electron itself. (Pauli, 2000, p. 15)

So, if one takes certain macroscopic, phenomenological special relativistic effects – for example, canonically – the contraction of rods and dilation of clocks (discussed in detail in later sections of this Element), the thought is that it would be legitimate to explain those effects in terms of the micro-constituents of the systems under consideration. As a matter of practical fact, however, we might lack an understanding of the physics of such micro-constituents, or it might be that to work out which such physics is experimentally intractable (consider, e.g., the number of degrees of freedom in statistical mechanics, often thereby requiring recourse to thermodynamics). For this reason, Brown and Pooley (2004) advance what they call a *truncated Lorentzian pedagogy*:

> In order to predict, on dynamical grounds, length contraction for moving rods and time dilation for moving clocks, Bell recognised that one need not know exactly how many distinct forces are at work, nor have access to the detailed dynamics of all of these interactions or the detailed micro-structure of indi-vidual rods and clocks. It is enough, said Bell, to assume Lorentz covariance of the complete dynamics – known or otherwise – involved in the cohesion of matter. We might call this the truncated Lorentzian pedagogy. (Brown & Pooley, 2004, p. 7)

---

[39] This is closely related to the 'clock hypothesis', introduced in Section 10.

The suggestion is that we can offer a *partial* explanation of special relativistic effects via appeal to the Poincaré invariance of the dynamical laws. A full (untruncated) explanation is deferred.

7.2 Constructive and Principle Theories, Reprised

Recall from Section 4 that a *constructive theory* attempts to provide a detailed dynamical picture of what is microscopically going on, from which predictions for observable phenomena can be derived. A *principle theory*, by contrast, takes certain phenomenologically well-grounded principles, raises them to the status of postulates, and derives from them constraints on what the underlying detailed dynamical equations could be like, without attempting to give a fully detailed account of what those equations *are*. The Lorentzian pedagogy suggests (straightforwardly) that the detailed microdynamics associated with special relativistic systems would provide the constructive account of the behaviour of those systems. Here, indeed, is Bell circa 1992 on precisely this matter:

> If you are, for example, quite convinced of the second law of thermodynamics, of the increase of entropy, there are many things that you can get directly from the second law which are very difficult to get directly from a detailed study of the kinetic theory of gases, but you have no excuse for not looking at the kinetic theory of gases to see how the increase of entropy actually comes about. In the same way, although Einstein's theory of special relativity would lead you to expect the FitzGerald contraction, you are not excused from seeing how the detailed dynamics of the system also leads to the FitzGerald contraction. (Bell, 1992, p. 34)

Clearly, Bell is suggesting that the fundamental microdynamics governing physical systems can provide a constructive underpinning of (macroscopic) special relativistic effects. Brown and Pooley are fully on board with this lesson, but others – certain geometricians – have a very different story to tell.[40] To be concrete, here is Janssen's very different take on the constructive theory associated with Einstein's 1905 special relativity:

> Minkowski (1909) did for special relativity, understood strictly as a principle theory, what Boltzmann had done for the second law of thermodynamics. It turned special relativity into a constructive theory by providing the concrete model for the reality behind the phenomena covered by the principle theory. (Janssen, 2009, p. 40)

---

[40] The story is subtle when it comes to some advocates of a geometrical view – for example, Maudlin (2012). As we will see, Maudlin is also completely on board with this lesson from Bell, yet nevertheless maintains that geometry has a significant role to play in the explanation of physical effects and phenomena.

The idea is that it is Minkowski spacetime structure which affords the constructive underpinning of special relativity. The state of play at this point, then, can be summarised as follows:

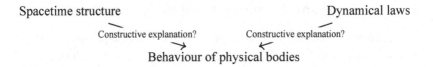

7.3 Arrows of Explanation

In order to make progress in this dispute regarding the constructive underpinnings of special relativistic phenomena, authors change focus: to whether spacetime structure *explains* the form of the dynamical laws governing the matter out of which our physical systems are constructed, or vice versa. Proponents of a 'dynamical' view *à la* Brown maintain something like this:

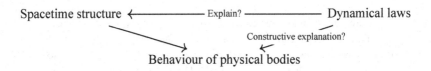

On the other hand, proponents of a 'geometrical' view *à la* Friedman, Janssen, or Maudlin maintain something like this:

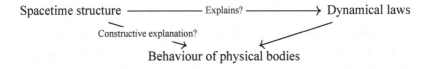

Our authors indeed recognise explicitly their disagreements as such. Here, again, is Janssen:

> Our central disagreement ... is a dispute about the direction of the arrow of explanation connecting the symmetries of Minkowski spacetime and the Lorentz-invariance of the dynamical laws governing systems in Minkowski spacetime. I argue that the spacetime symmetries are the *explanans* and that the Lorentz invariance of the various laws is the *explanandum*. Brown argues that it is the other way around. (Janssen, 2009, p. 29)

Brown agrees on the nature of this dispute, but (by now predictably!) does not think spatiotemporal geometrical explanations hold together:

Here we are at the heart of the matter. It is wholly unclear how this geometrical explanation is supposed to work. (Brown, 2005, p. 134)

As a matter of logic alone, if one postulates spacetime structure as a self-standing, autonomous element in one's theory, it need have no constraining role on the form of the laws governing the rest of the theory's models. So how is its influence supposed to work? Unless this question is answered, spacetime cannot be taken to explain the Lorentz covariance of the dynamical laws. (Brown & Pooley, 2004, p. 84)

Rather, Brown and Pooley propose to *reverse* the arrow of explanation, so that:

the appropriate structure is Minkowski geometry *precisely because* the laws of physics . . . are Lorentz covariant. (Brown & Pooley, 2004, p. 80)

There are three points to note on the proposal Brown and Pooley are making here. First, inasmuch as the position seeks to *reduce* spacetime structure to facts about the dynamical laws, arguably it is best understood as a modern-day form of *relationalism* (according to which spacetime is derivative – in some way or other – on material bodies and their behaviours)—see Pooley (2013).[41] Second, arguably, the view renders the connection between spacetime and dynamical symmetries *analytic*: spacetime structure *just is* an expression of dynamical symmetries (Myrvold, 2019; Acuña, 2016).[42] Third, if this view can indeed be made to hold together, then there is a clear sense in which spacetime symmetries (and structure) are *explained* by dynamical facts.[43]

To summarise so far, then: certain 'geometrical' authors such as Janssen maintain that spacetime structure *explains* the behaviour of matter and the symmetries of the associated laws. For Brown and Pooley, this is mysterious; they propose to reverse the arrow of explanation by *ontologically reducing* spacetime structure to an expression of the symmetries of the dynamical laws for material bodies, which (for them) are to be regarded as conceptually prior.[44]

---

[41] It has not escaped notice that this position is not neutral on the metaphysics of laws of nature: see Brown and Pooley (2004); Huggett (2009); Read (2020b).

[42] Brown is broadly on board with this claim – see Brown and Read (2021).

[43] For further discussion, see Read (2020b) and references therein.

[44] Several authors have reasonably asked whether one can articulate these laws without presupposing spacetime structure. I touched on this question in Section 6, but see, for example, Dewar (2020) for further discussion, as well as my discussion of Norton (2008) in what follows.

7.4 Geometrical Sub-views

In order to better understand the geometrical position, I now want to distinguish several different possible versions of this view:

Version A: Spacetime structure (e.g., the Minkowski metric field η_{ab} in special relativity) is ontologically autonomous and primitive, and (in some sense to be articulated) constrains the dynamical behaviour of matter.

Version B: Spacetime structure is not necessarily to be construed as ontologically autonomous and primitive, but is, rather, a *universal kinematical constraint* on possible physical theorising. (This position is close to that stated explicitly by Janssen (2009)). This kinematical constaint could be, for example,

1. a 'meta-law', in the sense of Lange (2007), or
2. a pragmatic restriction (more on which below).

Versions A and B.1 are both what I referred to in Read (2020a) as 'unqualified geometrical views', in the sense that both are subject to Brown and Pooley's challenge: *how is this geometrical explanation supposed to work?*[45] Version B.2 is, by contrast, a 'qualified geometrical view', in the sense that this charge does not apply to it: we can use (e.g.) η_{ab} to explain the behaviour of matter (including the symmetry properties of the laws governing matter), once we have restricted to a certain allowed class of laws (namely, those which are Poincaré invariant). We will see this view explicitly in a quote from Maudlin – so there is little doubt that Maudlin counts as a 'qualified geometrician'.

Before I get to Maudlin's views in more detail, though, I want to ask the following question: in what sense can a qualified geometrical approach offer a *constructive* explanation of the behaviour of the physical bodies under consideration? This is a good question, since not all proponents of a geometrical view profess to hypostatise spacetime (Janssen (2009), for example, explicitly does not do this). Since constructive explanations (i.e., explanations in terms of constructive *theories*: see Read (2020b)) make appeal to physical entities and goings-on, it seems to me that Janssen occupies an unstable position in both refusing to hypostatise spacetime yet nevertheless suggesting spacetime can offer constructive explanations of physical phenomena: in my view, the former is a necessary condition for the latter. Of course, though, this is not to say a non-hypostatised spacetime cannot offer *other* kinds of explanations

---

[45] For Brown on Version B.1, see Brown and Read (2021, p. 76).

of physical goings on – perhaps unificatory explanations, in the manner of Friedman (1974).[46]

What, then, of Maudlin? The following passage is revealing:

> Complete physical understanding of an equilibrium state would require a complete account of the internal structure of the rigid system, both its composition and the forces among its parts. But even absent such a detailed account, we can make some general assertions about rigid bodies in any Special Relativistic theory. The fundamental requirement of a relativistic theory is that the physical laws should be specifiable using only the relativistic space-time geometry. For Special Relativity, this means in particular Minkowski space-time. It is the symmetry of Minkowski space-time that allows us to prove our general result. (Maudlin, 2012, p. 117)

Note that the first sentence here is completely consistent with the Lorentzian pedagogy, so Maudlin wholly concurs with Brown and Pooley on this point. When Maudlin then writes that '[t]he fundamental requirement of a relativistic theory is that the physical laws should be specifiable using only the relativistic space-time geometry', this is also something to which the advocate of the dynamical approach should be able to assent (as a mathematical claim, at least). The remaining issues are (a) whether this spacetime structure is ontologically autonomous, and (b) whether it can offer a constructive explanation of the aforementioned effects. Advocates of the dynamical approach will assent to neither (a) nor (b), whereas Maudlin, I take it (albeit not in this quote!), *will* assent to both (a) and (b). Once one recognises Maudlin as a 'qualified geometrician', however, there does not seem to be anything profoundly problematic in his position (for further discussion, see Read (2020a)).

7.5 Norton's Challenge

Having clarified the different forms a geometrical view might take, I now want to turn to a different issue. Norton claims the whole idea of a 'dynamical approach' to spacetime is question-begging:

> Constructivists, such as Harvey Brown, urge that the geometries of Newtonian and special relativistic spacetimes result from the properties of matter. Whatever this may mean, it commits constructivists to the claim that these spacetime geometries can be inferred from the properties of matter without recourse to spatiotemporal presumptions or with few of them. I argue that the construction project only succeeds if constructivists antecedently presume the essential commitments of a realist conception of spacetime. (Norton, 2008, p. 821)

---

[46] For further discussions on all these issues, see Acuña (2016); Read (2020b).

Recall from Section 6 that, when constructing spacetime theories (on the Riemannian approach, at least), we begin by writing down a differentiable manifold M, before writing down certain additional (e.g.) metrical structure on that manifold. For example, recall that the spacetime structure of special relativity (on the Riemannian approach) is $\langle M, \eta_{ab} \rangle$; the (Galilean) space-time structure of Newtonian mechanics is $\langle M, t_{ab}, h^{ab}, \nabla \rangle$. Norton's claim is that Brown must presuppose the manifold M in order to write down dynamical equations for matter fields (for these equations hold at spacetime *points*), and so to get his relationalism about metric structure off the ground. So Brown's approach fails, according to Norton, for it implicitly makes certain spatiotemporal presuppositions.

Is this fair? Let us consider two responses to Norton. The first is from Pooley, who accuses Norton of misunderstanding the scope of the dynamical project:[47]

> The advocate of the dynamical approach need not be understood as eschew-ing all primitive spatiotemporal notions (*pace* Norton, 2008). In particular, one might take as basic the 'topological' extendedness of the material world in four dimensions. (Pooley, 2013, p. 55)
>   [T]he project was to reduce chronogeometric facts to symmetries, not to recover the entire spatiotemporal nature of the world from no spatiotemporal assumptions whatsoever. (Pooley, 2013, p. 57)

Others have argued that it is unreasonable to say Brown does not have a rela-tional account of the manifold, as indeed seems to be exhibited in the following passages:

> In pre-quantum physics then, space-time points are perhaps best viewed not as entities in their own right, but as correlations or links between the individual degrees of freedom of distinct physical fields. (Brown, 1997, p. 68)

> The simplest (and to my mind the best) conclusion, and one which tallies with our usual intuitions concerning the gauge freedom in electrodynamics, is that the space-time manifold is a non-entity. (Brown, 2005, p. 156)

One might, however, regard these statements as mere promissory notes: how exactly is Brown to eliminate his apparent commitment to manifold points? Menon (2019) takes up this challenge, using the machinery of 'algebraic fields' to *show* that manifold points can be understood as 'structural properties of mat-ter', in line with the quote from Brown. This work has very recently been developed further by Chen and Fritz (2021) – but a more sceptical response

---

[47] See also Stevens (2020).

is given by Linnemann and Salimkhani (2021). One concern expressed in the latter of these articles is this: how does demonstrating the existence of a mapping between (i) theories in their traditional manifold setting, and (ii) these theories formulated in terms of algebraic fields, actually resolve Norton's challenge? For this, one would surely need to argue that the formulation in (ii) is *metaphysically prior* to the formulation in (i) – but how would any such argument proceed?

These debates are ongoing. But what we can say, in light of the recent writings of *inter alia* Pooley and Menon, is that it is not clear whether Norton's charges against the dynamical approach find their mark.

8 The Conventionality of Simultaneity

Having presented the genesis of special relativity, several different ways in which one might understand the content of the theory, and the general architecture of the dynamical/geometrical debate, in the coming sections, I will introduce and chart the space of possible responses to some important special relativistic paradoxes and conceptual conundrums. I will begin with one of the most long-standing: the question of whether simultaneity is *conventional* in special relativity. We have seen in Section 4 some hints as to what this might mean; before explaining this in full detail, however, I must recall a better-known special relativistic phenomenon: the *relativity* of simultaneity.

8.1 The Relativity of Simultaneity

Recall the set-up introduced in Einstein's discussion of distant simultaneity in his 1905 article. Suppose one bounces a light ray from mirror A to mirror B, then back again to mirror A, as per Figure 4. Which point on the worldline of mirror A is simultaneous (according to a clock at A) with the 'bounce' point B_2 on the worldline of mirror B (according to a clock at B)? As we have already seen, Einstein stipulated the following natural answer to this question:

$$t_B(B_2) = t_A(A_1) + \frac{1}{2}(t_A(A_3) - t_A(A_1)). \tag{77}$$

This is the Einstein–Poincaré clock synchrony convention. If we apply this in all frames, then the *relativity of simultaneity* – which means adjudications on simultaneity will vary from inertial frame to inertial frame so that simultaneity is not an invariant of the relevant transformations – follows, as can be seen in Figure 14. Here, we consider a new coordinate system G in which our set-up (consisting of the two mirrors A and B and a bouncing light ray) is moving uniformly; by applying the Einstein–Poincaré synchrony convention in this frame, one finds *tilted* simultaneity hyperplanes. So, if we understand simultaneity à

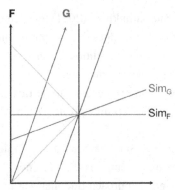

Figure 14 The Einstein–Poincaré clock synchrony convention in two
co-moving frames *F* and *G*, and the respective simultaneity surfaces Sim_F
and Sim_G

la Einstein, then the frame-relativity of simultaneity follows. But could it be
that, *even in one particular frame*, there is no fact about which point on the
worldline of mirror *A* is simultaneous with point B_2 on the worldline of mirror
B? One who thinks this would have to say there are no facts about simultaneity *even in one frame* – and thus these can be fixed by convention only. This
is the *conventionality of simultaneity*, which is conceptually distinct from the
relativity of simultaneity.

8.2 The Conventionality of Simultaneity

One of the first authors to explore systematically the possibility of other simultaneity conventions was Reichenbach in *The Philosophy of Space and Time*
(1958). Reichenbach maintained that we are free to make stipulations different from those of the Einstein–Poincaré convention about which point on the
worldline of mirror *A* is simultaneous with event B_2 on the worldline of mirror
B. To reflect this, he generalised Einstein's simultaneity relation by replacing
the factor of $1/2$ in (77) with an ϵ-factor, such that $\epsilon \in [0, 1]$:

$$t_B(B_2) = t_A(A_1) + \epsilon(t_A(A_3) - t_A(A_1)), \qquad 0 < \epsilon < 1. \tag{78}$$

Reichenbach's underlying thought was this: nothing in the formal structure of
special relativity fixes which synchrony convention we must use; it is, rather,
an additional input choice. This indeed squares with the way in which we have
already seen that Einstein understood the matter of distant clock synchrony in
special relativity.

How would the description of physical goings-on change if one were to
deploy a non-standard (i.e., $\epsilon \neq 1/2$) simultaneity convention in the rest frame
of the set-up? The answer is illustrated in Figure 15: simultaneity hyperplanes

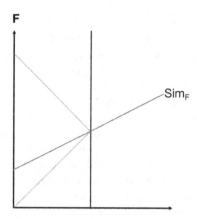

Figure 15 The $\epsilon = {}^1/_4$ convention in a frame F

in this convention will be *tilted*. Moreover, if we choose, for example, $\epsilon = {}^1/_4$, *simultaneity is still frame-relative* – that is, simultaneity hypersurfaces will still shift on transforming to frames co-moving with the original frame (assuming the same convention is used in the moving frame). Finally, any $\epsilon \neq {}^1/_2$ will mean the one-way speed of light is *not* isotropic.[48]

Why did Reichenbach bound ϵ by 0 and 1? Here is Brown on this question:

> I will have more to say about this Reichenbach factor ϵ shortly, but note that it is widely assumed that ϵ must be restricted to the closed set $[0, 1]$ . . . This is to ensure that in one direction light does not propagate backwards in time. It is often claimed that such a possibility would violate the fundamental canons of causality, but it is a hum-drum experience for airline travellers flying East across the International Date Line.
>
> I can testify, having flown from New Zealand to both North and South America, that arriving before you left is survivable! . . . Come to think of it, every telephone call from, say Australasia to the UK, involves a signal arriving before it left, and no one seems the worse for it. (Brown, 2005, p. 97)

Brown is stressing that we are free to coordinatise space and time in any way we please; even if a particular coordinatisation yields descriptions of physical events according to which there is (say) communication backwards in time, this will not lead to logical catastrophe. Therefore, although choosing $\epsilon \notin [0, 1]$ might yield just such descriptions, this is not *per se* problematic. This point is surely correct, yet one might feel Brown has missed something. Huggett hits the nail on the head here when he writes:

---

[48] The conventionality of simultaneity as discussed here is closely related to the fact that it is not possible to measure the one-way speed of light (Salmon, 1977).

Now of course we are logically free to coordinatize as we please, and so
we can assign, in principle, the same 'time' coordinate to any pair of points
we wish. Indeed, in the sense that coordinates are just labels for points, we
could attach absolutely any numbers to any points we liked. At certain points
(e.g., *PR*, 20, 97) Brown seems to mean nothing more by 'convention', but
surely this sense has little philosophical import.

A more weighty issue that motivates conventionalism is that of the status of spacetime geometry. The realist-minded about geometry will evaluate
different choices of coordinates according to how well they express the
geometric properties of the spacetime manifold. Of course, even if the manifold were a substance, with intrinsic geometric structure, then we could
still assign coordinates as we chose without affronting logic; but if there
are intrinsic facts of the matter about the geometry of spacetime then some
coordinates are 'better' than others. (Huggett, 2009, pp. 410–11)

Here is how I would put the point. It is of course uncontroversial that we
can coordinatise space and time in any way we please, and that descriptions of
physical events may be counter-intuitive or unnatural in some such coordinati-
sations. However, theories come endowed with laws with certain symmetries,
and the question is: to what extent do such symmetries fix (i.e., leave invariant –
see Section 5) certain notions – most relevantly for us in this section, simultaneity? Note that, in fact, it does not matter whether one has a 'dynamics-first'
view such as that of Brown or a 'geometry-first' view such as that of Friedman
in order to make this point. In both cases, the issue is: given those symmetries,
which notions are or are not well defined?[49]

Moving on from these issues, let us explore the ramifications of choosing
non-standard (i.e., $\epsilon \neq 1/2$) simultaneity conventions. Once one recognises the
possibility that $\epsilon \neq 1/2$ (however one takes the quantity to be bounded), an
array of *different* possible means of 'spreading time through space' arise. I will
focus on two, which I will call the 'Reichenbach-I' and 'Reichenbach-II' synchrony conventions. Let us begin with the former. Suppose we send a light
ray out in both directions with an $\epsilon = 1/4$ convention. Simultaneity surfaces
will not be flat, and there will be a preferred position in the reference frame.
This is represented by the line in Figure 16 marked '$\epsilon = 1/4$', bent at *A*. About
A, the description of the one-way speed of light is isotropic, but highly non-
homogeneous due to the preferred point. (On one natural understanding, C_2
and B_2 are simultaneous from the point of view of *A* but not from the point
of view of *C*, so what counts as simultaneous is not just frame-dependent, but

---

[49] Brown (2005, p. 20) also claims simultaneity is conventional in Newtonian mechanics –
however, the same criticisms would apply to that claim.

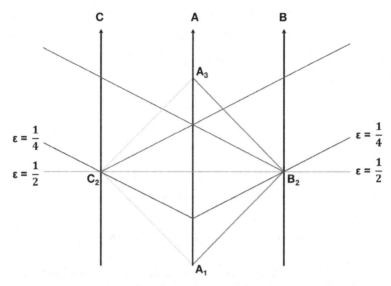

Figure 16 $\epsilon = {}^{1}/_{2}$ and $\epsilon = {}^{1}/_{4}$ Reichenbach-I conventions

position-dependent. A second natural understanding would have it that C_2 and B_2 are simultaneous *tout court* – but then there is something metaphysically privileged about A, which might seem mysterious.)

One objection to the Reichenbach-I synchrony convention is due to Torretti (1983, ch. 7). Call a timescale (i.e., an assignment of temporal coordinates to spacetime points) *inertial* just in case, relative to that timescale, free bodies have (or would have) constant velocities. Then an assignment of temporal coordinates as per the Reichenbach-I convention does not define an inertial timescale. To see this, consider a free body which crosses A's worldline. As the particle moves from one side of this worldline to the other, it (according to this way of spreading time through space) accelerates instantaneously – in spite of the fact that no force is acting on it. Given this, we can say that, when one adopts non-standard synchrony on the Reichenbach-I convention, the resulting frames of reference are not inertial frames (recalling Knox's functional definition of inertial frames given in Section 1), for they implicate free bodies in arbitrary accelerative motions.

Turn now to the Reichenbach-II synchrony convention. In this case, we set coordinated values of ϵ on either side of (in our example) A's worldline, such that no 'bend' arises in the simultaneity hypersurfaces. Suppose, for example, that we set $\epsilon = {}^{1}/_{4}$ on one side, then we set $\epsilon' := 1 - \epsilon = 1 - {}^{1}/_{4} = {}^{3}/_{4}$ on the other side. This will yield flat simultaneity surfaces (Figure 17). Around A, space will be anisotropic but homogeneous: light travels faster in the rightwards direction. Note that Torretti's objection does not apply in this case.

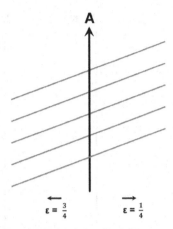

Figure 17 The Reichenbach-II convention

We have already seen that the description of the selfsame physical events can change, depending upon one's choice of simultaneity convention. Indeed, the derivation of the Lorentz transformations assumes standard ($\epsilon = {}^1/_2$) synchrony; adopting non-standard synchrony would require changing, *inter alia*:[50]

- The form of the Lorentz transformations.
- Length contraction and distances in a frame (typically a rod will contract differently when moving in different directions).
- Time dilation.
- How fast something moves relative to a reference frame.

Of course, though, empirically accessible quantities will have to stay the same (otherwise our synchrony convention would make an observable difference and no longer be a convention!). For example, the time read by two clocks when reunited after a 'twin paradox' journey will have to be the same, given any synchrony convention (Section 10).

8.3 Arguments against Conventionality

Since the possibility of the conventionality of simultaneity in special relativity was first raised, a number of different arguments have been presented to the effect that, in fact (and in spite of the foregoing discussions), simultaneity is *not* conventional in this theory. These arguments intimate that if one attends sufficiently carefully to the conceptual architecture of the theory, one will find only one simultaneity convention is permitted (typically, $\epsilon = {}^1/_2$ synchrony). Here, I will focus on two of the best-known such arguments:

---

[50] For details here, see Anderson, Vetharaniam, and Stedman (1998); Winnie (1970).

1. Arguments from slow clock transportation.
2. Malament's 1977 (purported) proof of non-conventionality.

8.3.1 Slow Clock Transport

The thought underlying the idea of synchrony by slow clock transport is this. Take two clocks, A and B, which are initially spatiotemporally coincident and synchronised. Now transport B infinitesimally slowly away from A. In such a scenario, the internal workings of the clock should not change, so the clocks (the thought goes) should continue to tick in step after B has been transported away from A.[51] In turn, this recovers standard synchrony.

The idea of using slow clock transport to establish a privileged simultaneity convention goes back (at least) to Eddington (1924) (although Eddington did not actually *endorse* this proposal). There are, however, a number of concerns with the approach, which have since been articulated. One is that the whole idea is question-begging because until the clocks are synchronized, there is no way of measuring the one-way velocity of the transported clock. In order to tackle this concern, Bridgman (1967, p. 26) used the 'self-measured' velocity, determined by using the transported clock to measure the time interval. However – in fact, like Eddington – he did not see this scheme as contradicting the conventionality thesis:

> What becomes of Einstein's insistence that his method for setting distant clocks – that is, choosing the value $1/2$ for ϵ – constituted a 'definition' of distant simultaneity? It seems to me that Einstein's remark is by no means invalidated. (Bridgman, 1967, p. 66)

The point is that using the slow clock method to synchronise distant clocks *is itself just another synchrony convention*. It is also, of course, completely irrelevant for clocks which are *not* originally transported away from one another in this way.

8.3.2 Malament's 1977 Theorem

I will now dedicate some attention to a theorem proven by Malament (1977), which was (and continues to be) interpreted by many as demonstrating unequivocally that simultaneity is *not* conventional in special relativity, and that only the $\epsilon = 1/2$ convention is allowed. As Brown puts it, Malament's proof is

---

[51] Note that here the 'clock hypothesis' – which I will discuss in detail in Section 10 – is invoked implicitly.

a result which virtually single-handedly managed to swing the orthodoxy within the philosophy literature from conventionalism to anticonventionalism. (Brown, 2005, p. 98)

The content of Malament's result is this. He claims to prove that the simultaneity relation $S(\cdot, \cdot)$ picked out by the standard ($\epsilon = 1/2$) convention is the only such relation

(a) which is invariant under all *O-causal automorphisms* (i.e., maps from Minkowski spacetime to itself preserving the lightcone structure and mapping the worldline of some observer O to itself),

(b) which is an equivalence relation,

(c) for which there exist world points p and q, one of which is on O's worldline and one of which is not, such that $S(p, q)$, and

(d) which is not the universal relation.

That is, Malament considers a world with only one inertial observer O, along with the causal (i.e., lightcone) structure of special relativity. He then considers the simultaneity relations which can be defined from this structure – that is, which respect the symmetries of this structure, which are known as the 'O-causal automorphisms' (if a symmetry relation were not to respect the symmetries of this structure, then it would – by the mantra of Section 5 – presuppose implicitly further structure, which is *ex hypothesi* prohibited), and shows that, subject to the further aforementioned (supposedly innocuous – but see, e.g., Grünbaum (2001); Janis (2018) for for discussion and criticism) constraints, this picks out uniquely the standard synchrony relation as the simultaneity relation which O would be able to use in order to 'spread time through space'.

What exactly *are* the O-causal automorphisms? They include all and only:

1. Translations along O.
2. Scale expansions.
3. Reflections about a hypersurface orthogonal to O.
4. Spatial rotations.

Visually, from left to right, these transformations are presented in Figure 18 (based upon Norton, 1992, p. 226). The idea is this: given an inertial worldline O in Minkowski spacetime, there is only one simultaneity relation which an observer represented by the wordline could define – namely standard synchrony. Any other simultaneity relation would not be invariant under O-causal automorphisms and so (to repeat) would imply a commitment to further spatiotemporal structure beyond that of Minkowksi spacetime. One prominent author who gives exactly this line of argument is Friedman:

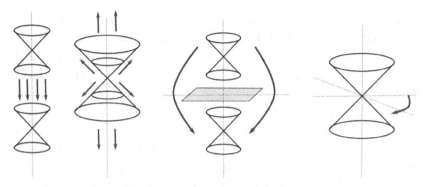

Figure 18 The *O*-causal automorphisms

> So we cannot dispense with standard simultaneity without dispensing with
> the entire conformal structure of Minkowski space-time. Second, it is clear
> that if we wish to employ a nonstandard [simultaneity] we must add fur-
> ther structure to Minkowski space-time. . . . This additional structure has no
> explanatory power, however, and no useful purpose is served by introducing
> it into Minkowski space-time. Hence the methodological principle of parsi-
> mony favors the choice of Minkowski space-time, with its 'built-in' standard
> simultaneity, over Minkowski space-time plus any additional nonstandard
> synchrony.
>
> These considerations seem to me to undercut decisively the claim that the
> relation of [simultaneity] is arbitrary or conventional in the context of special
> relativity. (Friedman, 1983, p. 312)

Friedman's point is that, in order to articulate non-standard synchrony conventions in a given frame in special relativity, one must introduce extra structure.
But, just as the extra structure in Newtonian spacetime (i.e., persisting points
of absolute space – see Section 5) is unnecessary to state the laws of Newtonian mechanics, so too is this extra structure otiose in the relativistic case. Thus,
Friedman is stating that while we *could* articulate non-standard synchrony conventions in a given frame, this would involve introducing extra structure, and
we have an Occamist norm to not do so (cf. Dasgupta, 2016). *This* is the import
of Malament's result for Friedman.

Not all authors agree with Friedman. Brown's response, perhaps predictably,
is very different:

> Why should we consider defining simultaneity just in terms of the limited
> structures at hand in the Grunbaum–Malament construction, namely an
> inertial world-line *W* and the causal, or light-cone structure of Minkowski
> space-time? (Brown, 2005, p. 100)

The thought is this: in the real world, there are *multiple* observers, each with
an associated worldline. What is wrong with saying *O* is to use the standard

simultaneity relation of O' – which need not be a standard simultaneity relation for O? Malament's proof, the thought goes, would have relevance only in the impoverised (and utterly counterfactual!) case in which only one inertial observer exists in a background Minkowksi spacetime. (See here also Janis, 2018.)

In fact, however, Brown's qualms run deeper than this: in the Malament world, it is not obvious that we have enough physical structure to set up coordinates *at all* (how, operationally, is one to 'spread time through space' with only one worldline – that of O?). There would, for example, be no way to set up 'radar coordinates' in such a world. (Not only this, but in fact stronger: it is not obvious that Brown – with his views that spacetime geometry is ultimately to be regarded as a codification of dynamics – will regard the Malament world as coherent to begin with!) So, given an operational understanding of coordinates (recall Section 4), it is not clear that it is legitimate to speak of simultaneity relations *at all* in that world. And in the actual world, there are many observers and much physical structure, which should afford *ample* opportunity to define non-standard simultaneity relations for O. Either way, Malament's proof seems to fail to show what is claimed.

For what it is worth, I find Brown's reasoning here convincing. But it is helpful to recall the different possible understandings of the content of special relativity (Section 6) in order to understand why the issue of the conventionality of simultaneity continues to propel authors in different directions. If one understands (as on the third option) special relativity to *just be* a theory of Minkowski spacetime and what is derivable therefrom, then the Malament–Friedman line that simultaneity is not conventional in special relativity (because only standard synchrony is definable using only one observer and said structure) looks more plausible. But if one has the second understanding, according to which special relativity has to do with Poincaré invariant material laws, then arguably Brown's position becomes the more plausible (here, there is no limit to the number of material bodies involved). Interestingly, if one takes the *first* understanding, according to which special relativity essentially amounts to the content of Einstein's 1905 paper, then there is a sense in which simultaneity is *not* conventional in the theory, for standard synchrony is baked into its axioms! This highlights that there can be both theory-*external* notions of conventionalism – which additional, super-empirical, assumptions to insist upon when building a theory? – and theory-*internal* notions of conventionalism – having fixed a theoretical edifice, what is definable uniquely therefrom and what is not?

Let me close this section with one broader thought. Famously, Quine, in his critique of the analytic/synthetic distinction, maintained that 'the lore of our fathers is . . . a pale grey lore, black with fact and white with convention. But I have found no substantial reasons for concluding that there are any quite black threads in it, or any white ones' (Quine, 1951). If correct, this would imply that there is no clean distinction between the (supposedly) empirically motiv- ated inputs in Einstein's 1905 derivation of the Lorentz transformations (e.g., his two postulates) and the (supposedly) conventional inputs (e.g., standard synchrony).

> **Question:** How plausible is Quine's position in the context of special relativity?

9 Frame-Dependent Effects

The phenomena of time dilation, length contraction, and the relativity of sim- ultaneity are often presented as the bread and butter of special relativity. However, there are good reasons for doubting the reality of these phenom- ena, for they are *frame-dependent* effects which do not admit of a description liberated from coordinate systems. So: are these truly physical effects or not?

9.1 Time Dilation

I will begin with time dilation: the famous special relativistic result that 'mov- ing clocks run slow'. It is easy to demonstrate time dilation directly from Einstein's two postulates: in a frame moving uniformly with respect to the light clock set-up Einstein presented at the beginning of his 1905 paper (Figure 4), the light will still travel with velocity c, but will now have to traverse the hypotenuse of a triangle – meaning the time between ticks will be greater.

The result can also be derived directly from the Lorentz transformations. Considering two coordinate systems related by a Lorentz boost in the positive x-direction, we have, where $\beta := {}^v/c$,

$$c\Delta t' = \gamma (c\Delta t - \beta \Delta x), \tag{79}$$

$$\Delta x' = \gamma (\Delta x - \beta c\Delta t), \tag{80}$$

$$\Delta y' = \Delta y, \tag{81}$$

$$\Delta z' = \Delta z. \tag{82}$$

Setting $\Delta x = 0$ in the first of these Lorentz transformations, we have $\Delta t' = \gamma \Delta t$. Thus, given a clock stationary in one frame, that clock will tick more slowly in a Lorentz-boosted frame.

But here is the rub: time dilation seems to arise because the time elapsed between ticks on a clock is *frame-relative*. So it seems that one 'gets a clock to slow down' merely by changing one's own frame of reference; but, in so doing, one clearly does nothing at all to the clock itself. (In other words, one need only perform a passive rather than an active transformation in order for time dilation to manifest itself – recall Section 2.) This line of thought seems to suggest that time dilation is not a real *physical* effect, but is a 'merely perspectival' one. Moreover, whether or not a clock moving in a given direction runs slow relative to any given frame depends upon how distant clocks are synchronised in that frame. Hence, conventionalists about simultaneity should also, for consistency, be conventionalists about time dilation – and this might reasonably further undercut any thought that time dilation is a 'real' phenomenon.

9.2 Length Contraction

Le me turn now to length contraction. Like time dilation, this phenomenon can be derived from Einstein's two postulates, as well as directly from the Lorentz transformations. This time, I will skip directly to the second. Consider again a boost in the positive x-direction. Combining (79) and (80), we have

$$\Delta x' = \gamma \Delta x - \beta c \Delta t' - \beta^2 \gamma \Delta x. \tag{83}$$

Setting $\Delta t' = 0$, we have

$$\Delta x' = \gamma \Delta x \left(1 - \beta^2\right). \tag{84}$$

But $\gamma^{-2} = 1 - \beta^2$, so

$$\Delta x' = \frac{1}{\gamma} \Delta x. \tag{85}$$

So, given a rod stationary in one frame, the distance between the ends of that rod at a given time will be smaller in a Lorentz-boosted frame.

Once again, there are worries here regarding perspectivalism and conventionalism. Length contraction seems to arise because the length of a rod is *frame-relative*. So it seems that one 'gets a rod to contract' merely by changing one's own frame of reference; but, in so doing, one clearly does nothing at all to the rod itself. This line of thought seems to suggest length contraction is not a real *physical* effect, but is a 'merely perspectival' one. Moreover, note that the length of a given object in a given frame depends upon the synchrony scheme for distant clocks in that frame – if (and only if) the object is moving relative to the frame in question. Hence, conventionalists about simultaneity should also, for consistency, be conventionalists about lengths of moving bodies – and this might reasonably further undercut any thought that length contraction is a 'real' phenomenon.

9.3 Bell's Rockets

We have already seen the relativity of simultaneity in the previous section, so I will skip an explicit discussion of that phenomenon here. Rather, I will turn now to the question of whether frame-dependent *explanations* in special relativity are – or can be – legitimate (as contrasted with the question of whether frame-dependent *phenomena* are physically real.) One of the most famous places in which frame-dependent explanations come to the fore is a thought experiment due to Bell (again in his article 'How to Teach Special Relativity'), regarding two rockets:

> Three small spaceships, *A*, *B* and *C*, drift freely in a region of space remote from other matter, without rotation and relative motion, with *B* and *C* equidistant from *A*.
> On reception of a signal from *A*, the motors of *B* and *C* are ignited and they accelerate gently.
> Let the ships *B* and *C* be identical, and have identical acceleration programmes. Then (as reckoned by the observer in *A*) they will have at every moment the same velocity, and so remain displaced one from the other by a fixed distance. Suppose that a fragile thread is tied initially between projections from *B* and *C*[, and that] it is just long enough to span the required distance initially. (Bell, 2004, p. 67)

Question: Does the string in Bell's rocket thought experiment break? Why, or why not?

Take a couple of minutes to think about this question before proceeding. As Bell explains, the answer to the question is this:

> If [the rope] is just long enough to span the required distance initially, then as the rockets speed up, it will become too short, because of its need to Fitzgerald contract, and must finally break. It must break when, at a sufficiently high velocity, the artificial prevention of the natural contraction imposes intolerable stress.
> Is it really so? This old problem came up for discussion once in the CERN canteen. A distinguished experimental physicist refused to accept that the thread would break, and regarded my assertion, that indeed it would, as a personal misinterpretation of special relativity. We decided to appeal to the CERN Theory Division for arbitration, and made a (not very systematic) canvas [*sic*] of opinion in it. There emerged a clear consensus that the thread would **not** break! (Bell, 2004, pp. 67–8)

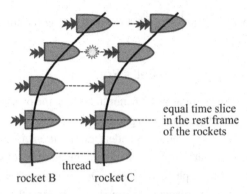

equal time slice
in the rest frame
of the rockets

thread

rocket B   rocket C

Figure 19 The Bell rocket set-up

So, the string breaks, as illustrated also in Figure 19 (based upon that by Maudlin (2012)). But let us think about the different explanations for *why* the string breaks which might be offered from different frames of reference:

- From the point of view of the control tower *A*, the breakage happens as a result of length contraction of the string.
- From the point of view of the first rocket *B*, the breakage happens as the second rocket moves progressively further away (due to the relativity of simultaneity – draw a spacetime diagram!).
- From the point of view of the second rocket *C*, the breakage happens as the first rocket lags further behind (due to the relativity of simultaneity – draw a spacetime diagram!).

All of these points should make sense (though I will return shortly to the question of whether frame-relative explanations in general are legitimate). So why so much confusion in the CERN theory division about whether the string would snap? The Bell rocket scenario is peculiar, in the following sense. If one were to begin with two rockets stationary with respect to one another and boost to a uniformly accelerating frame in special relativity (a 'Rindler frame'), one would find that the rockets do *not* have the same accelerations in this frame, at any given time. This difference in accelerations would mean the rockets move closer to one another as they accelerate, thereby implementing the length contraction effects. This does *not* happen in the Bell rocket scenario – so the rest frame of *A* is *not* a Rindler frame. This difference is illustrated in Figure 20 (based upon Weiss (2017)): the first represents the Bell rocket set-up; the second represents two rockets in a Rindler frame. Clearly, these two physical set-ups are different!

In other words, the point is this: many presented with this puzzle assume that, as the rockets accelerate, the rocket-string-rocket system length contracts

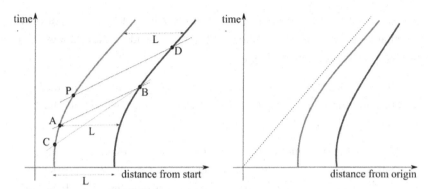

Figure 20 Left: The Bell rocket scenario, tilted simultaneity surfaces superimposed. Right: Two rockets in a Rindler frame

(from the point of view of the control tower *A*), so the string does not snap. However, *by stipulation*, in the Bell rocket scenario, the rockets maintain at all times equal spatial distance between them, in *A*'s frame. This means the rockets exert an ever-greater force on the string, ultimately meaning the latter will snap. In Bell's scenario, the string connecting the rockets is weak: it breaks under only a small applied force and is unable to keep the rockets together. If, however, the string were infinitely strong, then it would contract as the rockets accelerate, thereby pulling the rockets together: they would form a *Rindler pair*.

Having settled what can be so confusing about the Bell rocket example, let us return to our three frame-dependent accounts of why the string breaks in Bell's original scenario. Maudlin repudiates such explanations:

> The surface contradiction between these three accounts of why the thread breaks illustrates that frame-dependent narrations of events in Relativity can be misleading. There is one set of events, governed by laws that are indifferent to which coordinate system might be used to describe a situation. In each frame-dependent account, the interatomic forces in the thread play a role in determining exactly when the thread breaks. But how that role is described in a particular reference frame depends critically on which frame is chosen. (Maudlin, 2012, p. 120)

Question: What, exactly, is misleading about frame-dependent accounts of special relativistic phenomena?

9.4 Assessing Frame-Dependent Effects

Up to this point, we have witnessed frame-dependent effects such as time dilation and length contraction and seen arguments to the effect that these phenomena are 'merely perspectival' or conventional. We have also seen, in the context of the Bell rocket scenario, that one can find in the literature different attitudes towards the legitimacy of frame-dependent explanations. This means are two questions are in play:

1. Are frame-dependent *explanations* of physical phenomena legitimate?
2. Are frame-dependent *effects* – for example, length contraction and time dilation – 'physical'?

As we have seen, Maudlin disavows frame-dependent explanations (of, e.g., the Bell rocket result), for different explanatory accounts will be offered in different frames. But what exactly is wrong with availing oneself of such explanations? Why does a lack of univocity imply illegitimacy? Maudlin instead prefers coordinate-independent, *geometrical* explanations ('geometrical' in the sense that they make direct appeal to spacetime geometry), as is evident in passages such as the following:

> At first I followed standard presentations, making extensive use of coordinates and coordinate transformations. Bit by bit, class after class, reference to coordinates dropped away, leaving the fundamental geometry open to inspection. (Maudlin, 2012, p. ix)

Note, in particular, that in this passage Maudlin is:

1. Committing to a geometrical understanding of special relativity.
2. Disavowing frame-dependent explanations.

The thought is that only invariant structures – for example, the structure of Minkowski spacetime in special relativity – should feature in genuine explanations. Whatever one makes of this, it is clearly going to be anathema to, for example, Brown, for whom such invariant spacetime structures are just a codification of the symmetry properties of the dynamical equations governing matter, written in coordinate bases (Section 7).

Let us turn now to the second question: are frame-dependent effects 'physical'? To make progress in answering this question, let me say provisionally that a phenomenon associated with a coordinate transformation is *physical* just in case that transformation relates physically distinct states of affairs. So:

- Global Galilean boosts are physical in Newtonian spacetime.
- Global Galilean boosts are not physical in Galilean spacetime.
- Global Lorentz boosts are not physical in Minkowski spacetime. (Recall: Minkowski spacetime has no standard of rest.)
- *Local* Galilean boosts are physical in Galilean spacetime. (Consider Galileo's ship.)

- *Local* Lorentz boosts are physical in Minkowski spacetime. (Consider a constant-velocity-transformation version of Bell's rockets – this is what Maudlin calls 'physical length contraction'.)

The moral is this. The physicality of a coordinate effect (by the preceding definition of 'physicality') is crucially dependent upon

(a) the amount of spacetime structure presupposed, and
(b) whether the associated coordinate transformations are applied globally (i.e., to the whole universe) or locally (i.e., to subsystems of the universe).

Local transformations can effect genuine physical change, even if the particular *mode of description* of that change is frame-dependent (recall again Bell's rockets).

9.5 Fragmentalism

Within the metaphysics literature, there is a stronger view than that articulated at the end of the previous subsection, to the effect that *all* frame-dependent effects can (in principle) be regarded as physically real. This view is known as 'fragmentalism' and was first articulated by Fine (2005) in the context of the philosophy of time. According to this view, 'the world is inherently perspectival', and 'the overall collection of facts, "über reality", includes pairs of mutually incompatible facts' (Lipman, 2020, p. 23). So, on this view in the context of special relativity, the totality of facts about the universe includes frame-dependent facts about (e.g.) lengths of rods and periods of clocks, which are mutually inconsistent.

It is important to be clear on the fragmentalist's commitments. As Lipman writes,

> The importance is that of marking a metaphysical realism about those variant matters. The relevant question is whether realism or antirealism is true about the frame-relative facts, that is, whether consideration of the special theory of relativity removes all frame-relative facts from one's metaphysical conception of reality: the Minkowskian answers yes, the fragmentalist answers no. (Lipman, 2020, p. 31)

That is, the fragmentalist does not deny the existence of coordinate-independent facts to do with (say) Minkowski spacetime; they simply admit further, frame-dependent facts into their ontology. I will leave it to the reader to decide what to make of fragmentalism in the context of special relativity;[52] here, however, are two questions the fragmentalist must address:

---

[52] For my own take, see Read (2022).

> **Question:** How to make sense of a 'disunified reality', according to which 'the totality of facts is incoherent'?
>
> **Question:** What does fragmentalism add to the considerations of physicality and subsystem–environment decompositions introduced in this section?

10 The Twin Paradox

From *Planet of the Apes* to *Ender's Game*, the twin paradox is a mainstay of twentieth-century science fiction. Qualitatively, the idea is this: consider two identical twins at rest on Earth. One twin takes an interstellar journey before returning to Earth while the other remains at home on Earth; on reunion, our twins find they have aged by different amounts. So far, this is just a *feature* of special relativity – the *paradox* is supposed to consist in the fact that, if one considers the same situation in the rest frame of the travelling twin, then it seems it should be the *Earthbound* twin who ages less (the situations are entirely symmetrical, or so it seems). So, how to resolve this paradox?

10.1 The Clock Hypothesis

Before I discuss the twin paradox any further, I need to introduce a crucial device in the foundations of spacetime theories: what is known as the *clock hypothesis*. Suppose we have two identical clocks built from Poincaré invariant matter fields, with one clock moving with uniform velocity with respect to the first. Will these clocks function identically in their rest frames? *Yes*, by the relativity principle. Now suppose we have two identical clocks built from Poincaré invariant matter fields, with one clock accelerating with respect to the first. Will *these* clocks function identically in their rest frames? *Not necessarily* – for the relativity principle holds for systems related by *Poincaré* transformations.

Another (more geometrical) way to make the point is this. Given two clocks A and B, if B moves at uniform velocity with respect to A, then if A correctly reads off the Minkowski spacetime interval $\int_{\gamma_A} ds$ along its worldline γ_A, then so too will B correctly read off the interval $\int_{\gamma_B} ds$ along its worldline γ_B, by the relativity principle. However, if B accelerates with respect to A, then the fact that A correctly reads off the Minkowski spacetime interval $\int_{\gamma_A} ds$ along its worldline γ_A does not guarantee that B correctly reads off the interval $\int_{\gamma_B} ds$ along its worldline γ_B. That this is so is an additional input assumption, which is the clock hypothesis. As Maudlin puts it, the hypothesis amounts to this:

> The amount of time that an accurate clock shows to have elapsed between two events is proportional to the Interval along the clock's trajectory between those events, or, in short, clocks measure the Interval along their trajectories. (Maudlin, 2012, p. 76)

One should not, however, simply assume that the clock hypothesis is foundationally unproblematic. In fact, to suppose *any* clock satisfies the clock hypothesis is misleading, for all clocks have a breaking point. As Eddington said nicely of an accelerating clock,

> We may force it into its track by continually hitting it, but that may not be good for its time-keeping qualities. (Eddington, 1966, p.64)

The point is this: whether a particular clock ticks in accordance with the spacetime metric is not a matter of stipulation or luck, but depends crucially on the constitution of the clock. For any given clock, no matter how ideal its performance when inertial, there will in principle be an acceleration-producing external force, or even tidal effects inside the clock, such that the clock 'breaks', in the sense of violating the clock hypothesis. Might it therefore not be more appropriate to speak of the clock *condition*? (Brown & Read, 2016, §III.C).

Regardless of what one thinks of this, what is uncontroversial is that, whenever we have accelerating clocks, the clock hypothesis/condition must be brought into consideration: is it satisfied or not? And what upshots does this have for the discussion at hand? In much of this section, in order to render the contours of philosophical discussion of the twin paradox as crisp as possible, I will simply *assume* the clock hypothesis – but it is important to remember that this principle lurks beneath the hood. I will flag it again explicitly where relevant.

10.2 The Twin Paradox

Without further ado, then, let us turn to a more quantitative presentation of the twin paradox. Consider two identical twins A and B, who are spatiotemporally coincident on Earth at some time. Twin B decides to make an out-and-back trip away from Earth, while Twin A stays home: see Figure 21. It is a basic feature of special relativity that, on returning to Earth, Twin B will have aged less than Twin A. This is easy to see by computing the proper time (which is the time read off by a clock in the rest frame of the observer under consideration, which will correspond to the integral of the metric interval along that observer's worldline, on the assumption of the clock hypothesis) along the worldline of each twin:

$$T_A = \int_o^p d\tau_A \qquad (86)$$

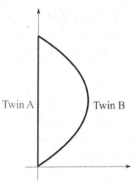

Figure 21 The twin paradox set-up

$$T_B = \int_o^p d\tau_B$$

$$= \int_o^p \left(1 - \left(\frac{dx}{d\tau_A} \right)^2 - \left(\frac{dy}{d\tau_A} \right)^2 - \left(\frac{dz}{d\tau_A} \right)^2 \right)^{\frac{1}{2}} d\tau_A$$

$$< T_A. \tag{87}$$

(Here, o and p are, respectively, the departure and reunion events of the two twins.) Note that the result of this computation is not relative to a particular frame—it is a *frame-independent fact* that Twin B has aged less than Twin A when they are reunited.[53] There is a temptation to appeal to time dilation in order to explain the twin paradox result, but (at least in the first instance) this should be resisted: we have already seen in the previous section that whether it is appropriate to appeal to time dilation will depend upon the frame of reference with respect to which one is describing the physical situation under consideration; moreover, there are choices of simultaneity convention which *eliminate* time dilation effects. Thus – again, as stressed previously – at the very least such accounts cannot be fundamental.

This result is certainly unexpected, but it is not yet a paradox. (Recall Quine's famous 1966 characterisation of a paradox: an apparently successful argument having as its conclusion a statement or proposition that seems obviously false or absurd.) But we can generate the paradox in the following way. We have seen that $T_A > T_B$ – and this is a *frame-independent result*. But if we were to boost to B's rest frame, the situation would look (it seems) exactly analogous. In that case, we would surely expect $T_B > T_A$. Assuming that $T_A \neq T_B$, this leads to a contradiction – and so to something more unavoidably classified as a paradox. So, *what breaks the symmetry between A and B?*

---

[53] This is a nice illustration of the sense in which drawing spacetime diagrams can be misleading – for B's path looks *longer* on the diagram, but is in fact *shorter* when we do the computation.

10.2.1 Inertial Frames

As a first response to the twin paradox, it is natural to appeal to inertial versus non-inertial frames (or, if one prefers language expunged of reference to frames, inertial versus non-inertial *trajectories*). Recall that Minkowski spacetime has the resources to distinguish straight ('inertial') from bent ('accelerating') trajectories. Suppose *A* is following an inertial trajectory relative to Minkowski spacetime structure; then (the thought would go), *B* is *not* following an inertial trajectory relative to the selfsame spacetime structure. Therefore, to boost to *B*'s rest frame would involve moving to a non-inertial frame, in which case, we should not expect the same laws of physics to apply. Thus, consideration of the structure of Minkowski spacetime allows us to break the symmetry between *A* and *B* and thereby resolve the paradox.

This reasoning on the basis on inertial frames is a plausible first reaction to the paradox – although ultimately we will see that it is not problem-free. Before I get onto that, though, we should recall from Section 1 that different authors have very different views on the nature of inertial frames. In particular, authors such as Brown might well be unhappy with the appeal to Minkowksi spacetime in the discussion of inertial frames. In light of this, we should ask: what role is Minkowski spacetime playing in the explanation? Could we excise it and just appeal to the inertial frames as picked out by the dynamics, rather than cashed out using geometrical notions? Indeed we can do this—here is how the account might go.

Suppose *A* is following an inertial trajectory – that is, it travels with uniform velocity in the inertial frames, as picked out by the dynamics (in one way or another – see Section 1). Then *B* is *not* following an inertial trajectory, for *B* accelerates with respect to *A*. Therefore, to boost to *B*'s rest frame would involve moving to a non-inertial frame, in which case, we should not expect the same laws of physics to apply. Thus (again, the thought might go) consideration of the inertial frames allows us to break the symmetry between *A* and *B* and thereby resolve the paradox.

My point here is really a simple one: one can appeal to inertial frames in order to attempt to account for the twin paradox time differential, on both a 'geometrical' and 'dynamical' understanding of inertial frames. Fair enough – but is the account actually any good to begin with? One should be careful about making too much of the inertial/non-inertial distinction, for one can formulate twin paradoxes with

(i) equal accelerations, or
(ii) no accelerations at all!

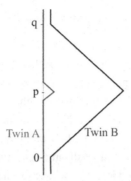

Figure 22 A version of the twin paradox in which both twins have identical acceleration profiles

Let me begin with the first case (here, I will draw on Maudlin's very elegant discussion of the twin paradox (2012, p. 82)). One can envisage a case where Twin *A* undertakes a 'mini-journey', but with the same acceleration profile, as per Figure 22. In this case, neither Twin *A* nor Twin *B* find themselves in inertial frames – nevertheless, on recombination, Twin *B* has still aged less than Twin *A*. Thus it seems it cannot be non-inertial motion *alone* which accounts for this result. On this issue, Maudlin writes the following:

> Both Rindler and Feynman point out that acceleration is objective in Relativity, just as it is in Newtonian absolute space and time and in Galilean space-time. This is true but irrelevant: the issue is how *long* the world-lines are, not how *bent*. (Maudlin, 2012, p. 83)

Let us turn to the second potential problem for inertial frame-based attempts to explain the twin paradox: the cases in which one has no accelerations at all. There are two such cases. The first involves not twin but *triplets*, *A* (the stay-at-home triplet), *B* (whose clock is initially synchronised with that of *A*, and who travels away from Earth with constant velocity), and *C* (who travels towards Earth with constant velocity, and who synchronises their clock with that of *B* on passing the latter). In this case, the time displayed by *C*'s clock will still be less than that displayed by *A*'s clock on recombination. Moreover, here, all three triplets are moving inertially – so can one really appeal to inertial versus non-inertial motion to account for this result?

> **Question:** How physical is this case, given that (presumably) some energy/momentum must be exchanged between Twin *B* and Twin *C*?

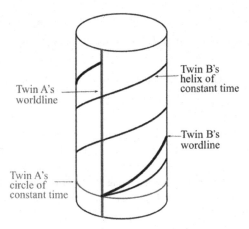

Figure 23 The twin paradox on a cylinder

The second 'no acceleration' case is particularly intriguing. Imagine our twins *A* and *B* find themselves on a spacetime of cylindrical topology, as per Figure 23.[54] In this case, Twin *A* stays home as before, whereas Twin *B* travels with constant velocity around the cylinder before rejoining Twin *A* on Earth. Again in this case, on recombination, Twin *B* will have aged less than Twin *A*. Since both twins are (it seems) moving inertially in this case, it would again seem one cannot appeal to the distinction between inertial and non-inertial motion in order to account for the time discrepancy between the clock readings of the twins.

In neither of these cases is there a straightforward way of appealing to the inertial/non-inertial distinction in order to account for the twin paradox time differential. That said, in the latter (i.e., the cylindrical spacetime case), per-haps there is still a difference between *A* and *B* – for only *A*'s worldline is aligned with the principal axis of the cylinder. In this case, at least, there *is* a preferred frame, allowing us to account for the cylindrical twin paradox time differential.

Exercise: Assess this response to the case of the cylindrical twin paradox.

What lessons should we take from these cases? Taken together, they suggest the twin paradox result cannot be accounted for solely in terms of the accel-

[54] Compare Weeks (2001, p. 587). For more on twin paradoxes in spacetimes of different topologies, see Luminet (2011).

erations of the twins. So, at this point – as we have seen in the quote from Maudlin – exploring other possible explanations is apposite.

10.2.2 Geometrical and Dynamical Explanations

On the twin paradox, Maudlin writes:

> The Twins 'Paradox' has inspired more confusion about Relativity than any other effect. The explanation of the phenomenon, in terms of the intrinsic geometry of Minkowski space-time and the Clock Hypothesis is exquisitely simple: clocks measure the Interval along their world-lines, and B's world-line between o and q is longer than A's. Period. There is nothing more to say. (Maudlin, 2012, p. 79)

It is certainly true that this kind of geometrical account of the twin paradox time differential faces no apparent counterexamples, as with the previously countenanced appeals to inertial frames. But how illuminating is it? Presumably, a 'dynamicist' (e.g., Brown) would find the spacetime explanation of the cylindrical twin paradox (and the equal-acceleration twin paradox) similarly otiose and would say, even if it is not an (operationalised) notion of inertial frames which accounts for the time differential, it is still *facts about the matter out of which the twins are built*, more generally construed, which account for the difference, rather than anything to do with spacetime geometry.

To summarise, the dialectic here between the 'geometrical' camp *à la* Maudlin and the 'dynamical' camp *à la* Brown proceeds as follows. An initial 'geometrical' thought might be that it is spacetime which grounds the distinction between inertial and non-inertial motion, and it is this distinction which can be appealed to in an explanation of the twin paradox time differential. Such a line of thought could be represented thus:

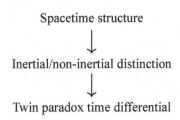

On the other hand, an initial 'dynamical' thought, as we have seen, would be that this appeal to spacetime is redundant and one can appeal directly to the inertial/non-inertial distinction (as, ultimately, given by facts about the dynamics) in order to account for the twin paradox time differential. Such a line of thought could be represented thus:

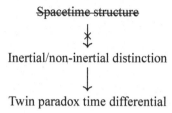

In light of our problem cases, however, we have seen it is difficult to maintain that appeal to the inertial/non-inertial distinction can account completely for the twin paradox result. In light of this, a revised 'geometrical' understanding (again, *à la*, e.g., Maudlin) would appear thus:

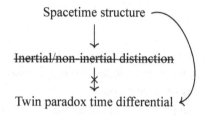

By contrast, a revised 'dynamical' thought would maintain that it is facts about dynamics which *directly* explain the twin paradox time differential; appeal to the inertial/non-inertial distinction is likewise recognised to be unnecessary here:

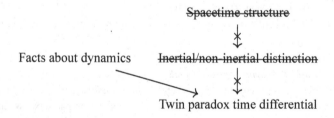

> **Question:** Which of the 'geometrical' or 'dynamical' approaches to the twin paradox is to be preferred, and why?

10.3 Frame-Relative Accounts

There are many purported 'explanations' of the twin paradox which appeal to *frame-relative structures*. (The situation is very similar to that of, e.g., Bell's rockets.) Here, I will present one of the most prominent of these, which appeals

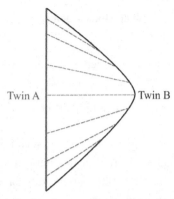

Figure 24 The standard twin paradox set-up, with Einstein–Poincaré
simultaneity hypersurfaces for Twin *B* superimposed

to simultaneity hypersurfaces in *B*'s rest frame.[55] I will then consider (in a con-
tinuation of the discussion presented in the previous section) the more general
question of the legitimacy of these accounts.

The account of the twin paradox time differential which appeals to the relativity of simultaneity proceeds like this. Consider the ($\epsilon = 1/2$) simultaneity
hyperplanes from the point of view of *B*'s rest frame. At the turnaround point,
there is a sudden swing in the hyperplanes, leading to 'lost time' relative to
A's worldline. The situation would be illustrated on a spacetime diagram as in
Figure 24. The claim, then, is that it is this 'lost time' which accounts for the
time differential between *A* and *B*. This seems fine (at least if one is Brown –
not if one is Maudlin!), but is the account a fundamental one? Here is Brown
on this question:

> *Explanations of synchrony-independent phenomena in SR that rely cru-
> cially on the relativity of simultaneity are not fundamental.* (A common
> example concerns the clock retardation effect, or 'twins paradox', where
> it is claimed that at the point of turn-around of the travelling clock, the
> hyperplanes of simultaneity suddenly change orientation and the resulting
> 'lost time' accounts for the fact that the clocks when reunited are out of
> phase. It is worth bearing in mind that the clock retardation effect, like any
> other synchrony-independent phenomenon in SR, is perfectly consistent with
> all the non-standard transformations . . ., including those which eliminate
> relativity of simultaneity.) (Brown, 2005, p. 105, emphasis in original)

---

[55] This particular proposal was first made by von Laue in 1913 (Miller, 1981).

I agree with Brown (who, on this front, would also agree with Maudlin). There are indeed three reasons such accounts of the twin paradox result should be regarded as non-fundamental:[56]

1. They are frame-relative.
2. They are convention-relative. (Debs & Redhead, 1996)
3. They apply only to certain versions of the paradox – for example, not to the cylindrical case.

To repeat: Maudlin *agrees* such accounts are non-fundamental, but also (as we have seen in the previous section) regards such accounts as thereby illegitimate. Thus, the difference between authors such as Brown on the one hand, and such as Maudlin on the other, *vis-à-vis* such frame-dependent accounts, can be summarised thus:

Brown-style: They are legitimate but non-fundamental.
Maudlin-style: They are illegitimate and non-fundamental.

10.4 General Relativity

It is sometimes claimed that, since the twin paradox scenario involves accelerations, we must appeal to general relativity to explain the result (at various stages, Einstein and Born made such claims: see Jammer (2006, p. 165)). Recall that general relativity is Einstein's theory of gravitation, completed in 1915, according to which spacetime structure is dynamical and can vary in the presence of matter. Consideration of accelerations afforded a crucial way into the theory for Einstein; my conjecture is that it is *this* role of the consideration of accelerations – as an heuristic for the *construction* of general relativity – which ultimately has led to the confused and incorrect claims that discussion of accelerations *requires* recourse to general relativity – which it emphatically does not! Any such claim indeed is confused, for:

1. Accelerations are *not* an essential feature of the twin paradox – as we have seen.
2. Special relativity *has the resources to distinguish accelerating from non-accelerating trajectories.* (Recall Section 5.)

---

[56] Those who do not accept that simultaneity is conventional in special relativity – recall Section 8 – would not accept (2). This, however, would not prevent them from accepting the conclusion, in light of (1) and (3).

Still, it is worth dissecting this reasoning a bit more, to see what is really wrong with it.

Consider the fictitious force terms one obtains by writing one's theories of physics in non-inertial frames of reference (we have seen explicit examples of these terms in Section 1 and Section 6). Call these terms 'inertial effect' terms. Einstein (1907) had an insight – now known as 'Einstein's equivalence principle' (see Lehmkuhl, 2021) – that such inertial effect terms are to be *identified conceptually* with terms representing gravitation (for further discussion here, see Lehmkuhl (2014)).

One *could* appeal to Einstein's equivalence principle to explain (accelerating versions of) the twin paradox: the accelerating twin is subject to a gravitational force. But – crucially! – note that this is really no better than the original (bad!) appeal to accelerations! Moreover, this approach is also in tension with a widespread methodology in the philosophy of physics: try to understand effects which arise in a given theory *in terms of that theory itself* – that is, without introducing notions which transcend that theory. Thus claims that one has to appeal to general relativity in order to account for the twin paradox result implicate one in a misunderstanding of (a) the equivalence principle, (b) the representational and descriptive capacities of special relativity (to repeat again: accelerations are perfectly meaningful here!), and (c) the necessity of accelerations for twin paradox effects. Best, then, to avoid such appeals when one is engaging in the philosophical and conceptual ramifications of the special theory.

References

Acuña, P. (2016). Minkowski spacetime and Lorentz invariance: The cart and the horse or two sides of a single coin? *Studies in History and Philosophy of Science Part B: Studies in History and Philosophy of Modern Physics, 55,* 1–12. https://doi.org/10.1016/j.shpsb.2016.04.002.

Anderson, R., Vetharaniam, I. & Stedman, G. (1998). Conventionality of synchronisation, gauge dependence and test theories of relativity. *Physics Reports, 295*(3), 93–180. https://doi.org/10.1016/S0370-1573(97)00051-3.

Barbour, J. B. (1989). *The discovery of dynamics: A study from a Machian point of view of the discovery and the structure of dynamical theories.* New York: Oxford University Press.

Barrett, T. W. (2015). Spacetime structure. *Studies in History and Philosophy of Science Part B: Studies in History and Philosophy of Modern Physics, 51,* 37–43. https://doi.org/10.1016/j.shpsb.2015.06.004.

Bell, J. S. (1992, Sep). George Francis FitzGerald. *Physics World, 5*(9), 31–5. https://doi.org/10.1088/2058-7058/5/9/24.

Bell, J. S. (2004). How to teach special relativity. In *Speakable and unspeakable in quantum mechanics: Collected papers on quantum philosophy* (2nd ed., pp. 67–80). Cambridge: Cambridge University Press. https://doi.org/10.1017/CBO9780511815676.011.

Belot, G. (2000). Geometry and motion. *British Journal for the Philosophy of Science, 51*(4), 561–95. https://doi.org/10.1093/bjps/51.4.561.

Berzi, V. & Gorini, V. (1969). Reciprocity principle and the Lorentz transformations. *Journal of Mathematical Physics, 10,* 1518–24. https://doi.org/10.1063/1.1665000.

Bridgman, P. W. (1967). *A sophisticate's primer of relativity.* London: Routledge and Kegan Paul.

Brown, H. R. (1997). On the role of special relativity in general relativity. *International Studies in the Philosophy of Science, 11*(1), 67–81. https://doi.org/10.1080/02698599708573551.

Brown, H. R. (2005). *Physical relativity: Space-time structure from a dynamical perspective.* Oxford: Oxford University Press.

Brown, H. R. & Pooley, O. (2001). The origin of the spacetime metric: Bell's 'Lorentzian pedagogy' and its significance in general relativity. In C. Callender & N. Huggett (eds.), *Physics meets philosophy at the Planck scale* (256–72). Cambridge: Cambridge University Press.

Brown, H. R. & Pooley, O. (2004). Minkowski space-time: A glorious nonentity. In D. Dieks (ed.), *The ontology of spacetime* (pp. 67–89). Amsterdam: Elsevier.

Brown, H. R. & Read, J. (2016). Clarifying possible misconceptions in the foundations of general relativity. *American Journal of Physics, 84*, 327. https://doi.org/10.1119/1.4943264.

Brown, H. R. & Read, J. (2021). The dynamical approach to spacetime theories. In E. Knox & A. Wilson (eds.), *The Routledge companion to philosophy of physics* (pp. 70–85). London: Routledge.

Cajori, F. (1934). *Sir Isaac Newton's mathematical principles of natural philosophy and his system of the world* (A. Motte, trans.). Berkeley: University of California Press.

Chen, L. & Fritz, T. (2021). An algebraic approach to physical fields. *Studies in History and Philosophy of Science Part A, 89*(C), 188–201. https://doi.org/10.1016/j.shpsa.2021.08.011.

Cheng, B. & Read, J. (2021). Why not a sound postulate? *Foundations of Physics, 51*(3), 1–20. https://doi.org/10.1007/s10701-021-00479-0.

Dasgupta, S. (2016). Symmetry as an epistemic notion. *British Journal for the Philosophy of Science, 67*(3), 837–78. https://doi.org/10.1093/bjps/axu049.

Debs, T. A. & Redhead, M. L. G. (1996). The twin 'paradox' and the conventionality of simultaneity. *American Journal of Physics, 64*, 384–92.

Dewar, N. (2019). Sophistication about symmetries. *British Journal for the Philosophy of Science, 70*(2), 485–521. https://doi.org/10.1093/bjps/axx021.

Dewar, N. (2020). General-relativistic covariance. *Foundations of Physics, 50*(4), 294–318. https://doi.org/10.1007/s10701-019-00256-0.

Dewar, N., Linnemann, N. & Read, J. (2022). The epistemology of spacetime. *Philosophy Compass, 17*(4). https://doi.org/10.1111/phc3.12821.

Earman, J. (1989). *World enough and spacetime*. Cambridge, MA: MIT Press.

Earman, J. & Friedman, M. (1973). The meaning and status of Newton's law of inertia and the nature of gravitational forces. *Philosophy of Science, 40*(3), 329–59. https://doi.org/10.1086/288536.

Eddington, A. (1924). *The mathematical theory of relativity*. Cambridge: Cambridge University Press.

Eddington, A. (1966). *Space, time and gravitation: An outline of the general theory of relativity*. Cambridge: Cambridge University Press.

Einstein, A. (1905a, January). Ist die Trägheit eines Körpers von seinem Energieinhalt abhängig? *Annalen der Physik, 323*(13), 639–41. https://doi.org/10.1002/andp.19053231314.

Einstein, A. (1905b, January). Über die von der molekularkinetischen Theorie der Wärme geforderte Bewegung von in ruhenden Flüssigkeiten suspendierten Teilchen. *Annalen der Physik, 322*(8), 549–60. https://doi.org/10.1002/andp.19053220806.

Einstein, A. (1905c, January). Über einen die Erzeugung und Verwandlung des Lichtes betreffenden heuristischen Gesichtspunkt. *Annalen der Physik, 322*(6), 132–48. https://doi.org/10.1002/andp.19053220607.

Einstein, A. (1905d, January). Zur Elektrodynamik bewegter Körper. *Annalen der Physik, 322*(10), 891–921. https://doi.org/10.1002/andp.19053221004.

Einstein, A. (1907, January). Bemerkungen zu derNotiz von Hrn. Paul Ehrenfest: Die Translation deformierbarer Elektronen und der Flächensatz. *Annalen der Physik, 328*(6), 206–8. https://doi.org/10.1002/andp.19073280616.

Einstein, A. (1919). What is the theory of relativity? *The Times.* Friday, 28 November.

Einstein, A. (1921). *Geometrie und erfahrung: Erweiterte fassung des festvortrages gehalten an der preussischen akademie der wissenschaften zu berlin am 27.januar 1921.* Berlin: J. Springer.

Einstein, A. (1935). Elementary derivation of the equivalence of mass and energy. *Bulletin of the American Mathematical Society, 41*(4), 223–30.

Einstein, A. (1954). The fundamentals of theoretical physics. In *Ideas and opinions* (pp. 323–35). New York: Bonanza Books.

Einstein, A. (1969). Autobiographical notes. In P. A. Schilpp (ed.), *Albert Einstein: Philosopher-scientist* (Vol. 1, pp. 1–94). Chicago, IL: Open Court.

Einstein, A. (1995). *Letter to Arnold Sommerfield, January 14, 1908* (M. J. Klein, A. J. Knox & R. Schulmann, eds.). Princeton, NJ: Princeton University Press.

Fine, K. (2005). Tense and reality. In *Modality and tense: Philosophical papers.* Oxford: Oxford University Press.

FitzGerald, G. F. (1889). The ether and the Earth's atmosphere. *Science, 13*, 390.

Friedman, M. (1974). Explanation and scientific understanding. *Journal of Philosophy, 71*(1), 5–19.

Friedman, M. (1983). *Foundations of space-time theories.* Princeton, NJ: Princeton University Press.

Galilei, G. (1967). *Dialogues concerning the two chief world systems* (S. Drake, trans.). Berkeley: University of California Press.

Giovanelli, M. (2014). 'But one must not legalize the mentioned sin': Phenomenological vs. dynamical treatments of rods and clocks in Einstein's thought. *Studies in History and Philosophy of Science Part B: Studies in History and Philosophy of Modern Physics, 48*(1), 20–44. https://doi.org/10.1016/j.shpsb.2014.08.012.

Giovanelli, M. (2021). Nothing but coincidences: The point-coincidence and Einstein's struggle with the meaning of coordinates in physics. *European Journal for Philosophy of Science, 11*(2), 1–64. https://doi.org/10.1007/s13194-020-00332-7.

Griffiths, D. J. (2013). *Introduction to electrodynamics* (4th ed.). Boston, MA: Pearson.

Grünbaum, A. (2001). David Malament and the conventionality of simultaneity: A reply. *Foundations of Physics, 40*(9–10), 1285–97. https://doi.org/10.1007/s10701-009-9328-3.

Heras, J. A. (1994, October). Electromagnetism in Euclidean four space: A discussion between God and the Devil. *American Journal of Physics, 62*(10), 914–16. https://doi.org/10.1119/1.17681.

Hertz, H. (1894). *Die prinzipien der mechanik.* Leipzig: J. A. Barth.

Huggett, N. (2000). Reflections on parity nonconservation. *Philosophy of Science, 67*(2), 219–41. https://doi.org/10.1086/392773.

Huggett, N. (2006). The regularity account of relational spacetime. *Mind, 115*(457), 41–73. https://doi.org/10.1093/mind/fzl041.

Huggett, N. (2009). Essay review: Physical relativity and understanding spacetime. *Philosophy of Science, 76*(3), 404–22. https://doi.org/10.1086/649814.

Huggett, N., Hoefer, C. & Read, J. (2022). Absolute and relational space and motion: Post-Newtonian theories. In E. N. Zalta (ed.), *The Stanford encyclopedia of philosophy* (Spring 2022 ed.). Metaphysics Research Lab, Stanford University. https://plato.stanford.edu/archives/spr2022/entries/spacetime-theories.

Jackson, J. D. (1998). *Classical electrodynamics* (3rd ed.). New York: Wiley.

Jammer, M. (2006). *Concepts of simultaneity: From antiquity to Einstein and beyond.* Baltimore, MD: Johns Hopkins University Press.

Janis, A. (2018). Conventionality of simultaneity. In E. N. Zalta (ed.), *The Stanford encyclopedia of philosophy* (Fall 2018 ed.). Metaphysics Research Lab, Stanford University. https://plato.stanford.edu/archives/fall2018/entries/spacetime-convensimul.

Janssen, M. (2009). Drawing the line between kinematics and dynamics in special relativity. *Studies in History and Philosophy of Science Part B: Studies in History and Philosophy of Modern Physics, 40*(1), 26–52. https://doi.org/10.1016/j.shpsb.2008.06.004.

Kitcher, P. (1989). Explanatory unification and the causal structure of the world. In P. Kitcher & W. Salmon (eds.), *Minnesota studies in the philosophy of science* (Vol. 13, pp. 410–503). Minneapolis: University of Minnesota Press.

Knox, E. (2013). Effective spacetime geometry. *Studies in History and Philosophy of Science Part B: Studies in History and Philosophy of Modern Physics, 44*(3), 346–56. https://doi.org/10.1016/j.shpsb.2013.04.002.

Knox, E. (2014). Newtonian spacetime structure in light of the equivalence principle. *British Journal for the Philosophy of Science, 65*(4), 863–80. https://doi.org/10.1093/bjps/axt037.

Lange, M. (2007). Laws and meta-laws of nature: Conservation laws and symmetries. *Studies in History and Philosophy of Science Part B: Studies in History and Philosophy of Modern Physics, 38*(3), 457–81. https://doi.org/10.1016/j.shpsb.2006.08.003.

Larmor, J. (1900). *Aether and matter*. Cambridge: Cambridge University Press.

Lehmkuhl, D. (2014). Why Einstein did not believe that general relativity geometrizes gravity. *Studies in History and Philosophy of Modern Physics, 46*, 316–26.

Lehmkuhl, D. (2021). The equivalence principle(s). In E. Knox & A. Wilson (eds.), *The Routledge companion to philosophy of physics* (pp. 125–44). London: Routledge.

Linnemann, N. & Read, J. (2021). *Constructive Axiomatics in Spacetime Physics Part I: Walkthrough to the Ehlers–Pirani–Schild Axiomatisation.* (Unpublished manuscript.)

Linnemann, N. & Salimkhani, K. (2021). *The Constructivist's Programme and the Problem of Pregeometry.* (Unpublished manuscript.)

Lipman, M. A. (2020). On the fragmentalist interpretation of special relativity. *Philosophical Studies, 177*(1), 21–37. https://doi.org/10.1007/s11098-018-1178-4.

Lorentz, H. A. (1892). De relative beweging van de aarde en den aether. *Koninklijke Akademie van Wetenschappen te Amsterdam, Wis-en Natuurkundige Afdeeling, Versalagen der Zittingen, 1*, 74–9. (Reprinted in English translation, 'The relative motion of the Earth and the ether'. In P. Zeeman and A. D. Fokker (eds.), *Collected papers*, pp. 219–23, The Hague: Nijhjoff, 1937.)

Lorentz, H. A. (1895). *Versuch einer thoerie der electrischen und optischen erscheinungen in bewegten körpern.* Leiden: Brill.

Luminet, J.-P. (2011). Time, topology, and the twin paradox. In C. Callender (ed.), *The Oxford handbook of philosophy of time* (pp. 528–45). Oxford: Oxford University Press.

Malament, D. (1977). Causal theories of time and the conventionality of simultaneity. *Noûs, 11*(3), 293–300. https://doi.org/10.2307/2214766.

Malament, D. (2012). *Topics in the foundations of general relativity and Newtonian gravitation theory*. Chicago, IL: University of Chicago Press.

Martens, N. C. M. & Read, J. (2020). Sophistry about symmetries? *Synthese, 199*(1–2), 315–44. https://doi.org/10.1007/s11229-020-02658-4.

Maudlin, T. (2012). *Philosophy of physics: Space and time*. Princeton, NJ: Princeton University Press.

Menon, T. (2019). Algebraic fields and the dynamical approach to physical geometry. *Philosophy of Science, 86*(5), 1273–83. https://doi.org/10.1086/705508.

Mercati, F. (2018). *Shape dynamics: Relativity and relationalism*. Oxford: Oxford University Press.

Michelson, A. A., & Morley, E. (1887). On the relative motion of the Earth and the luminiferous ether. *American Journal of Science, 34*(203), 333–45.

Miller, A. I. (1981). *Albert Einstein's special theory of relativity*. Reading: Addison–Wesley.

Minkowski, H. (1909). Raum und zeit. *Physikalische Zeitschrift, 10*, 104–11.

Myrvold, W. C. (2019). How could relativity be anything other than physical? *Studies in History and Philosophy of Science Part B: Studies in History and Philosophy of Modern Physics, 67*, 137–43. https://doi.org/10.1016/j.shpsb.2017.05.007.

Norton, J. D. (1992). Philosophy of space and time. In *Introduction to the philosophy of science* (pp. 179–231). Englewood Cliffs, NJ: Prentice-Hall.

Norton, J. D. (1993). General covariance and the foundations of general relativity: Eight decades of dispute. *Reports on Progress in Physics, 56*(7), 791–858.

Norton, J. D. (2008). Why constructive relativity fails. *British Journal for the Philosophy of Science, 59*(4), 821–34. https://doi.org/10.1093/bjps/axn046.

Norton, J. D. (2018). *Einstein for Everyone*. Pittsburg, PA: Nullarbor Press.

Norton, J. D. (2022). The hole argument. In E. N. Zalta & U. Nodelman (eds.), *The Stanford encyclopedia of philosophy* (Winter 2022 ed.). Metaphysics Research Lab, Stanford University. https://plato.stanford.edu/archives/win2022/entries/spacetime-holearg.

Pais, A. (1982). *Subtle Is the Lord: The Science and the Life of Albert Einstein*. New York: Oxford University Press.

Pauli, W. (2000). *Relativitätstheorie*. Berlin: Springer. (Originally published by B. G. Teubner in 1921; new annotation by Domenico Giulini.)

Pelissetto, A. & Testa, M. (2015). Getting the Lorentz transformations without requiring an invariant speed. *American Journal of Physics, 83*, 338–40.

Pitts, J. B. (2012). The nontriviality of trivial general covariance: How electrons restrict 'time' coordinates, spinors fit into tensor calculus, and $\frac{7}{16}$ of a tetrad is surplus structure. *Studies in History and Philosophy of Science Part B: Studies in History and Philosophy of Modern Physics, 43*(1), 1–24. https://doi.org/10.1016/j.shpsb.2011.11.001.

Pooley, O. (2013). Substantivalist and relationist approaches to spacetime. In R. Batterman (ed.), *The Oxford handbook of philosophy of physics* (pp. 522–86). Oxford: Oxford University Press.

Pooley, O. (2021). The hole argument. In E. Knox & A. Wilson (eds.), *The Routledge companion to philosophy of physics*. London: Routledge.

Quine, W. V. O. (1951). Two dogmas of empiricism. *Philosophical Review, 60*(1), 20–43.

Quine, W. V. O. (1966). *The ways of paradox*. New York: Random House.

Read, J. (2020a). Explanation, geometry, and conspiracy in relativity theory. In T. S. C. Beisbart & C. Wuthrich (eds.), *Thinking about space and time: 100 years of applying and interpreting general relativity* (Vol. 15, pp. 173–206). Basel: Birkhäuser.

Read, J. (2020b). Geometrical constructivism and modal relationalism: Further aspects of the dynamical/geometrical debate. *International Studies in the Philosophy of Science, 33*(1), 23–41. https://doi.org/10.1080/02698595.2020.1813530.

Read, J. (2022). Geometric objects and perspectivalism. In J. Read & N. J. Teh (eds.), *The philosophy and physics of Noether's theorems* (pp. 257–73). Cambridge: Cambridge University Press.

Read, J. (2023). *Background independence in classical and quantum gravity*. Oxford: Oxford University Press.

Read, J., Brown, H. R. & Lehmkuhl, D. (2018). Two miracles of general relativity. *Studies in History and Philosophy of Science Part B: Studies in History and Philosophy of Modern Physics, 64*, 14–25. https://doi.org/10.1016/j.shpsb.2018.03.001.

Read, J. & Cheng, B. (2022). Euclidean spacetime functionalism. *Synthese, 200*(6), 1–22. https://doi.org/10.1007/s11229-022-03951-0.

Reichenbach, H. (1958). *The philosophy of space and time*. Berkeley: University of California Press.

Reichenbach, H. (1969). *Axiomatization of the theory of relativity*. Berkeley: University of California Press.

Rigden, J. S. (1987). Editorial: High thoughts about Newton's first law. *American Journal of Physics, 55*(4), 297. https://doi.org/10.1119/1.15191.

Ryckman, T. (2017). *Einstein*. London: Routledge.

Salmon, W. C. (1977). The philosophical significance of the one-way speed of light. *Noûs, 11*(3), 253–92.

Salmon, W. C. (1984). *Scientific explanation and the causal structure of the world*. Princeton, NJ: Princeton University Press.

Saunders, S. (2013). Rethinking Newton's *Principia*. *Philosophy of Science, 80*, 22–48.

Stevens, S. (2020). Regularity relationalism and the constructivist project. *British Journal for the Philosophy of Science, 71*(1), 353–72.

Todd, S. L. & Menicucci, N. C. (2017). Sound clocks and sonic relativity. *Foundations of Physics, 47*, 1267–93.

Todd, S. L., Pantaleoni, G., Baccetti, V. & Menicucci, N. C. (2021). Particle scattering in analogue-gravity models. *Physical Review D, 104*(064035).

Torretti, R. (1983). *Relativity and geometry*. New York: Pergamon.

US Naval Observatory. (2022). *Introduction to calendars*. https://aa.usno.navy.mil/faq/calendars.

Van Camp, W. (2011). Principle theories, constructive theories, and explanations in modern physics. *Studies in History and Philosophy of Modern Physics, 42*, 23–31.

von Ignatowsky, W. (1911). Das relativitätsprinzip. *Archiv der Mathematik und Physik, 17*, 1–24.

Wallace, D. (2019). Who's afraid of coordinate systems? An essay on representation of spacetime structure. *Studies in History and Philosophy of Modern Physics, 67*, 125–36.

Wallace, D. (2020). Fundamental and emergent geometry in Newtonian physics. *British Journal for the Philosophy of Science, 71*(1), 1–32.

Weatherall, J. O. (2018). A brief comment on Maxwell(/Newton)[–Huygens] spacetime. *Studies in History and Philosophy of Modern Physics, 63*, 34–8.

Weatherall, J. O. (2021). Two dogmas of dynamicism. *Synthese, 199*, 253–75.

Weeks, J. R. (2001). The twin paradox in a closed universe. *American Mathematical Monthly, 108*(7), 585–90.

Weiss, M. (2017). *Bell's spaceship paradox*. http://math.ucr.edu/home/baez/physics/Relativity/SR/BellSpaceships/spaceship_puzzle.html.

Winnie, J. (1970). Special Relativity without One-Way Velocity Assumptions: Part I. *Philosophy of Science, 37*, 81–99.

Acknowledgements

I am very grateful to Harvey Brown, Patrick Dürr, Dennis Lehmkuhl, Niels Linnemann, Tushar Menon, Oliver Pooley, Nic Teh, and Jim Weatherall for by now many happy years of discussion on the foundations of special relativity. I also thank Marta Bielińska for producing many of the figures, Will Wolf for help with the bibliography, and Amelie Gilardi for correcting typos. Finally, I thank Sumana for tolerating my constant (and, presumably, quite irritating) worrying about when I am going to write this.

I dedicate this book to my son, Aditya.

Cambridge Elements ☰

The Philosophy of Physics

James Owen Weatherall

University of California, Irvine

James Owen Weatherall is Professor of Logic and Philosophy of Science at the University of California, Irvine. He is the author, with Cailin O'Connor, of *The Misinformation Age: How False Beliefs Spread* (Yale, 2019), which was selected as a *New York Times* Editors' Choice and Recommended Reading by *Scientific American*. His previous books were *Void: The Strange Physics of Nothing* (Yale, 2016) and the *New York Times* bestseller *The Physics of Wall Street: A Brief History of Predicting the Unpredictable* (Houghton Mifflin Harcourt, 2013). He has published approximately fifty peer-reviewed research articles in journals in leading physics and philosophy of science journals and has delivered over 100 invited academic talks and public lectures.

About the Series

This Cambridge Elements series provides concise and structured introductions to all the central topics in the philosophy of physics. The Elements in the series are written by distinguished senior scholars and bright junior scholars with relevant expertise, producing balanced, comprehensive coverage of multiple perspectives in the philosophy of physics.

Cambridge Elements $\equiv$

The Philosophy of Physics

Printed in the United States
by Baker & Taylor Publisher Services